THE
FIELD & STREAM
Wilderness
Cooking
Handbook

The Field & Stream Fishing and Hunting Library

The Field & Stream *Bowhunting Handbook* by Bob Robb
The Field & Stream *Deer Hunting Handbook*
  by Jerome B. Robinson
The Field & Stream *Firearms Safety Handbook* by Doug Painter
The Field & Stream *Shooting Sports Handbook* by Thomas McIntyre
The Field & Stream *Sporting Vehicles Handbook* by Slaton L. White
The Field & Stream *Turkey Hunting Handbook* by Philip Bourjaily
The Field & Stream *Upland Game Handbook* by Bill Tarrant

The Field & Stream *Baits and Rigs Handbook* by C. Boyd Pfeiffer
The Field & Stream *Bass Fishing Handbook* by Mark Sosin and
  Bill Dance
The Field & Stream *Fishing Knots Handbook* by Peter Owen
The Field & Stream *Fish Finding Handbook* by Leonard M. Wright Jr.
The Field & Stream *Fly Fishing Handbook* by Leonard M. Wright Jr.
The Field & Stream *Tackle Care and Repair Handbook*
  by C. Boyd Pfeiffer

THE
FIELD & STREAM

Wilderness Cooking Handbook

How to Prepare, Cook, and Serve Backcountry Meals

J. Wayne Fears

THE LYONS PRESS

Guilford, Connecticut
An imprint of The Globe Pequot Press

The Lyons Press is an imprint of The Globe Pequot Press.

Originally published as *Backcountry Cooking* by the East Woods Press, Fast & McMillan Publishers, Inc., copyright © 1980.

Printed in Canada

10 9 8 7 6 5 4 3 2 1

The Library of Congress Cataloging-in-Publication Data

Fears, J. Wayne, 1938–
    The field & stream wilderness cooking handbook: how to prepare, cook, and serve backcountry meals/J. Wayne Fears.
        p. cm.
    Previously published: Charlotte, N.C.: East Woods Press, c1980 under title: Backcountry cooking.
    ISBN 1-58574-355-0
    1. Outdoor cookery. I. Title: Field and stream wilderness cooking handbook. II. Fears, J. Wayne, 1938– Backcountry cooking. III. Field and stream. IV. Title.
TX823.F422 2001
641.5'78—dc21   2001029647

To four of my favorite backcountry companions, my children

JEFF, CARLA, STEVE, AND CHRIS

Contents

Foreword   *ix*
Introduction   *1*

1. Mastering the Backpack Stove   5
2. The Art of Building a Cooking Fire   11
3. Cooking Without Utensils   21
4. Cooking with Aluminum Foil   25
5. The Versatile Dutch Oven   31
6. Reflector-Oven Baking   43
7. The Sheepherder's Stove   49
8. Bannock—Bread of the Wilderness   63
9. Sourdough—Bread of Legend   71
10. Make Your Own Jerky   79
11. Trail Foods You Can Make Ahead   87
12. Making Your Own Dried Food   93
13. Smoking Food   101
14. Cooking with Charcoal   109
15. Bean Hole Cooking   119
16. Making Water Safe for Drinking   123
17. Backcountry Drinks   129
18. Cooking at High Elevations   133

Appendices
1. List of Suppliers   135
2. List of Recipes   137

Index   *141*
More Wilderness Recipes   *145*

Foreword

When I was younger and tougher (in other words, broke and ignorant), I enjoyed roughing it when I hunted and fished with my friends. Our camps were bare-bones affairs, and I still remember an old surplus Army sleeping bag that had no warming properties whatsoever and a canvas tent (also surplus) that leaked like a sieve in a light mist. We preferred the romance of the open fire (we didn't have a gas stove), so cooking usually meant impaling channel cats on green sticks and then squatting and coughing over a smoky fire.

On one of those trips along Virginia's Shenandoah River for smallmouth bass, our patience with the quality of the evening meal finally reached the breaking point. Our self-elected camp cook had obvious talent, but one way or another grit always found its way into every meal, prompting one member of the group to proclaim late one night, "Why is it that every time you cook I need to get my teeth re-enameled?"

Enjoying a meal outdoors is one of the great pleasures in life—as well as one of the great disasters. You may feel that such calamities are an essential part of the hunting and fishing experience.

Maybe.

But there's a better way—and it starts with this remarkable book. The author, with whom I hunted a number of years ago, is one of the most savvy outdoor writers at work today, a complete outdoorsman who has hunted and fished throughout North America.

J. Wayne Fears grew up in Alabama, where he learned cooking and other outdoor skills from his dad, who was a trapper. He is a professional wildlife manager with degrees from Auburn University and the University of Georgia as well as a freelance outdoor writer with more than 3,000 magazine articles and 14 books under his belt. He also happens to be the editor of *Rural Sportsman* magazine.

As you might expect from such experience, J. Wayne Fears has eaten many meals by the light of a campfire. The recipes found in *The Field & Stream Wilderness Cooking Handbook* are marvels of simplicity and nutrition. More important, the first few chapters are worth the price of admission alone. If I had known what Wayne knows about cooking in the wild when I started out, I could have saved myself—and my friends—a lot of misery. (But then we wouldn't have the great stories that now enliven our evening fires.)

Outdoor cooking books are usually a mix of the philosophical and the practical. All too often the mix is wrong. But Fears gets it just right. For example, "Mastering the Backpack Stove" manages to be at once a succinct history of this remarkable tool as well as practical guide to its use. And in "The Art of Building a Cooking Fire," he acknowledges that too few hunters and fishermen know how to build a proper fire for *cooking*. Then he tells you how to do it right, and includes a terrific chart that evaluates campfire wood. Is it easy to split? Is it easy to burn? Does it produce heavy smoke? This is great stuff.

But that's not all. "Cooking Without Utensils" and "Cooking with Aluminum Foil" are simply great examples of knowledge put to practical use. He also pulls the famous but now hardly used sheepherder's stove back from oblivion.

Every page of this indispensable book reflects a lifetime spent in the wild. It is hard-won experience. Pay attention. Your stomach will thank you.

—SLATON WHITE
Editor
Field & Stream

Introduction

Welcome to one of the most enjoyable aspects of the great outdoors—wilderness "backcountry" cooking. This book was written with three purposes in mind: to record some old ways of cooking that in our modern rush are slowly disappearing; to show how basic cooking skills can convert any fireplace, wood stove, or patio into an alternate-energy cooking site; and to pass along some recipes that are used by those with less complicated life styles.

The reader will be quick to see that this is not a book just for backpackers, even though many people think the word *backcountry* is reserved only for backpackers. This book discusses at length the use of open campfires and the use of dead wood for fuel. The current environmental movement promotes the ethic of no fires, no ashes, no fire rings, and no charcoal sticks—a good policy in most areas. But there are those who get into little-used areas and cannot accomplish the cooking task at hand with a single burner backpack stove. They must use open fires, but must be careful to leave campsites as natural as they found them.

Someone once said that the chief difference between humans in the wilderness and wild animals in the wilderness is that humans can control fire for their use. Unfortunately, the art of building a fire and using it properly for cooking is dying as a new breed of outdoor enthusiasts enters the backcountry. During the past few years I have had the task of looking for lost forest visitors. On several occasions I have found people wandering hungry, cold, and scared, after discarding all their camping gear and using every match, desperately trying to start a fire. This book addresses those who need to learn the basics of fire building.

Many of these chapters show the homeowner that loss of electrical power or gas does not doom one to unsavory meals. The fireplace can be used for cooking with aluminum foil, the Dutch oven,

1

Clockwise from bottom left: backpack stove, reflector oven, sheepherder's stove, Dutch ovens, charcoal grill, smoker.

and the reflector oven. Anything that can be cooked on the sheepherder's stove can be cooked on the home wood stove. Smoking, drying, and charcoal cooking can be enjoyed at home, at the cabin, or in the wilderness.

This great country of ours was explored and settled by people who used these or similar methods of cooking. It surprises many fireplace owners to learn that the fireplace was the site of all cooking in the 1700s. The Dutch oven, which was the main cook kit for the Lewis and Clark expedition, works just as well today as it did then, and is still being used by a surprising number of people.

Perhaps one of the most fascinating things about backcountry cooking techniques is their versatility. I have used the little backpack stove to feed surprised students in cross-country ski classes, canoe trips into the Okefenokee Swamp, and hikes above timberline in the Rockies. My reflector oven has fascinated hunters from log cabin camps in Pennsylvania to boat camps in Alaska. My sheepherder's stove has been set up in fireplaces of long-abandoned farmhouses, in tents in British Columbia, and once on a raft in the Pacific Northwest. The same fascination can be found with primitive cooking skills, that is, cooking over an open fire without the aid of utensils or modern conveniences. On several occasions I have had only this simple method of cooking on which to depend. I came through well fed, and to this day, occasionally delight in attending a rendezvous of the modern mountain men, where primitive cooking is all that is permitted.

Those who spend their lives working in wild places have a warm spot in their heart for these cooking skills that have kept them well fed and healthy. I hope that as you read this book you will develop the same fondness for these backcountry skills.

Many of the good foods prepared in the backcountry were used throughout the history of our country. Native Americans and other travelers have long depended upon jerky. Today, it is sold in many different types of stores and made in wood stoves at remote ranches. And the delightful aroma of sourdough bread cooking recalls the gold miners in Alaska who lived on this staff-of-life. Today it has become fashionable to keep a sourdough starter and to cook homemade bread. Trail foods, old and new mixtures, are the topic of conversation around the sales counters of many outfitting stores, and are finding their way into school and work lunch boxes.

In many of the chapters of this book, I have included recipes from my own collection that can be tried on your home stove or by the cooking methods that I suggest. However, not all of the recipes are my own doing. Some I got from old-timers who have spent a lifetime on horseback in the mountains, some from trappers who cannot read or write, some from home economists who test in the best kitchens to be found, and some from backyard chefs who just like good food.

CHAPTER 1

Mastering the Backpack Stove

One of the major factors that has made backpacking popular has been the development of the little backpack stoves. Not too many years ago if you wanted to hike back into a wilderness area you had to cook over an open fire or take along a stove that might or might not work. Today that has all changed.

Backpack stoves fall into five basic fuel types—butane, kerosene, alcohol, propane, and white gasoline. For many years butane stoves were the leaders because they are simple to use. All you do is screw a butane cartridge onto a stove unit; you do not have to carry fuel containers because the cartridges serve that purpose. However, these stoves have their drawbacks. Butane, a gaseous hydrocarbon, is considered a fair weather fuel. It has zero pressure at 35°F and will not vaporize at 20°F or below, resulting in very limited use in cold temperatures. A second problem is that the heat output of butane stoves declines as the fuel supply in the cartridge drops. This means the lower the fuel supply, the longer it will take you to prepare a meal. Since you cannot change cartridges on many of the butane stoves until they are empty, you must suffer through some slow cooking. Furthermore, the cartridges must be packed out. Too many popular backpack campsites, far into the backcountry, have been littered with empty butane cartridges.

The white gas stoves were, for several years, a second choice for most backpackers. The stoves were hard to get started and it was often difficult to regulate the flame. Even with these problems I used a little Primus 71 stove all over the world because it would burn, with some cursing and coaxing, at low temperatures. Then a new product was introduced which relieved the miseries of backpack cooking. I accidentally learned of the product while it was still being tested.

During the winter of 1975, I was participating in an outdoor education program at the Environmental Learning Center near Isabella, Minnesota. One day, we were out on a cross-country skiing expedition when we were shown a new white gas stove that was being tested for the Coleman Company. It was 30°F below zero when we stopped for lunch, and I had my doubts if the strange little stove would work at all, let alone boil water. Yet, to my surprise, we had hot tea in five minutes. I was sold.

Since that cold day, Coleman has come out with a line of Peak I lightweight backpack stoves that makes lightweight-stove cooking a breeze. This is a product that has earned its way to the top, and I have had the opportunity to use it under many varied conditions. It is, in my opinion, the best of the backpack stoves.

The modern backpack stove can turn freeze-dried food into welcome meals with little effort. *Photo courtesy of the Coleman Co. Inc.*

Since most backpackers enjoy one-pot meals from freeze-dried foods, most backpack cook kits consist of a pot or two and a cup. The popular Campways backpack cook set is a two-person set consisting of a one and one-half quart pot, a Teflon-coated pan, two plates, and two plastic drinking cups. I am still using a World War II U.S. Army mountain cook kit that consists of an aluminum fry pan fitted over two pots with wire bails. In it are a plastic cup, a spoon, and a pot scrubber.

For carrying extra liquid fuel, I use a fuel container made of anodized spun aluminum and carry a small funnel for pouring.

One of the first things the owner of a new backpack stove should do before shoving off into some remote corner of backcountry is to cook a meal or two on the patio at home. Learn how to use the new stove properly and experiment with freeze-dried foods. Modern stoves and foods are relatively easy when compared with what was available years ago, but it still takes a little bit of experience to turn out properly prepared food.

The backpack stove is a good backup stove for home use in the event of a power or gas loss. Use the stove where there is ample ventilation such as on the patio or carport. Also remember fuel for the stove is extremely flammable. Do not use it in the house. With proper use it can be as excellent a home stove as it is a backcountry one.

Cooking on the backpack stove can be as easy as boiling water if you use freeze-dried food. Freeze-drying is a revolutionary way to prepare foods, which removes only water and locks in flavor and goodness. The result is food that is as fresh as the day it was made, and its weight is reduced by as much as 90 percent. There are several companies marketing these foods specially packaged for one, two, or four people.

The secret to making freeze-dried foods taste good is to follow the instructions to the letter. If the product calls for hot water, use boiling hot water. If cold water is called for, the colder the water the better. If you cook the food too long it will taste mushy, and if not long enough, it may crunch a little and taste flat. The variety of specially packaged freeze-dried foods available is almost endless. Choices such as beef stew, chili, rice and chicken, beef stroganoff, eggs, applesauce, shrimp Creole, ice cream, green peas, carrots, and corn, just to mention a few, are available at your backpack store or by direct mail from the supplier. (See list of suppliers at the back of this book.)

Expense is the chief disadvantage in using specially packaged freeze-dried foods. You may be surprised by how much you will pay for a week's supply of freeze-dried backpack foods. The best way to hold down the cost is to shop for freeze-dried and dehydrated foods at your local grocery store. They are packaged in larger sizes for home use but can be repackaged into individual servings in resealable plastic bags for trail use. Check all ingredients needed to reconstitute the food. It is much simpler to stay with those products needing only the addition of water, eliminating several mixing processes and an array of pots and pans.

Macaroni and cheese, spaghetti, mashed potatoes, soy bacon bits, beef, chicken dinners, or soup are some of the foods you may want to package yourself.

For vegetables, one-cup vegetable soups are good. There are also several good rice dishes available.

For desserts, instant puddings made with instant milk are quick and easy. Dried fruits such as apples, apricots, and peaches can also be tasty. To have pancakes, drop biscuits, and fish batter, take along a package of Bisquick.

Breakfast can consist of hot Tang, hot cocoa, instant grits, instant oatmeal, and other cereals.

When you organize for a trip, place each of the prepackaged items you have in plastic bags into a larger bag by meals. This procedure requires planning of meals, thus eliminating searching throughout your backpack for food items, and it saves time. Label each meal bag so that you can quickly find "Dinner First Day." Keep unused food in the meal bag from which it came, and when you return home revise your menu and quantity based on the meal bags. It is surprising how much you can learn about meal planning this way.

If you use commercially packaged backpack foods, you can get a free meal planner from various companies. These planners can give you advice on planning meals for a trip of up to seven days. However, even when using their specially packaged foods, I would suggest that you bag your food by meals.

Since freeze-dried foods and dehydrated foods both require water for cooking, the availability of water at your meal site is an important part of planning your trip. Many people take these types of foods into areas assuming that they can use a local water supply. When the water is not there, they find themselves in trouble. People in this predicament, who eat the dry food anyway, without water, risk suffering acute dehydration. Be sure of your water supply or take plenty of water with you.

The Art of Building a Cooking Fire

The growing number of outdoorsmen who do not know how to build a fire amazes me more every year. Many shade tree environmentalists will jump to their feet and be quick to say this is great—there will be fewer forest fires and black fire rings to scar the woods. This may be so, but there is a place in the backcountry where safe and sane fires are a necessity; it behooves all of us to know the proper way to go about building a fire. There also is a place for wood stoves and fireplaces in our homes. We may all live to see the day when we flip the switch or cut on the gas and nothing will happen. Then the cooking fire will suddenly become very important.

THE CAMPFIRE

The first step in building a fire is to select a safe place for it, assuming there is not an established fireplace. Pick a site that is at least fifteen feet from tents, green trees, dry grass, or anything else that could catch fire or be damaged from the heat or sparks. Also, be sure to check overhead. Many times an overlooked tree branch can hang directly over the fire area. Be careful when selecting a fire site not to build a fire over roots or peat moss. Fire can burn and smolder within roots and pop up as a wildfire around the base of the tree. Peat moss can burn underground for days and start a major fire long after you have moved on to a new campsite. If there is ground cover such as pine needles or leaves at your fire site, clear it away, exposing the bare earth for ten to fifteen feet. Put the cleared mate-

11

The keyhole fire makes an excellent cooking fire.

rial in a pile nearby for use in restoring your site to its original condition when breaking camp.

Most newcomers to open-fire cooking have the misconception that the larger the fire, the better it cooks. However, the best cooking fire is a small fire consisting mostly of hot coals. The best-known cooking fire is the keyhole fire. It is simply rocks laid in a keyhole outline filled with tinder and firewood. In the round part of the keyhole a fire is kept going to provide a supply of hot coals for the narrow part, where the cooking takes place. This type of fire warms as well as cooks. As more coals are needed in the cooking portion, take a stick and pull hot coals from the fire. A word of caution about using rocks: porous rocks gathered from streambeds or wet ground may contain enough water to build up steam and explode when heated in a fire.

If you find it necessary to dig a pit or trench for a fire, be sure to set aside the dirt you remove to refill the hole upon departure.

Once you have selected a safe site for your fire and have constructed a keyhole rock ring, the next chore will be to gather an adequate supply of firewood. The first rule of firewood gathering is to never cut anything green. Use the dead sticks that are in the immediate area of your camp as a first choice, and then go after larger dead trees that may still be standing.

Knowing which wood burns best is the mark of an experienced fire builder. Softwoods like pine, spruce, and fir are easy to ignite because they are resinous. They burn rapidly with a hot flame; however, a fire built entirely of softwoods, just like a fire of scrap paper, burns out so quickly that it requires frequent attention and replenishment. This characteristic of softwoods can be a boon if you want a quick warming fire or a short fire that will burn out before you go to bed.

For a longer fire it is best to use softwoods in combination with the heavier hardwoods such as ash, beech, birch, maple, and oak. These hardwood species burn less vigorously and with a shorter flame. Oak gives the shortest and most uniform flames and produces steady, glowing coals. When you have several oak logs burning in your campfire, you can settle back for a steady show of flame.

The best woods for cooking are hardwoods because their coals last longer and do not give food a resinous flavor.

A good rule to follow in gathering wood for an overnight fire is to gather twice as much as you think will be necessary. It surprises most beginning campers to discover how much wood a campfire can burn in one evening.

If you are caught in a rainstorm, look for standing dead wood. It is often much drier than wood lying on the ground. However, most dense hardwood logs are dry toward the center even after several days of rain. By splitting these logs, dry firewood can be found. Medrick Northrop, a friend of mine who teaches survival classes, always amazes his students by pulling a hardwood log out of a lake and splitting it to use for firewood. His fires always start right up.

After a sizable supply of firewood has been stacked, the next task is to find a supply of tinder to get the fire going. Tinder can be found wherever you are located. Some examples are old birds' nests, birch bark, dry cedar bark, dry evergreen twigs, sagebrush bark, dead lower twigs found on evergreen trees, and, perhaps best of all, the rich resinous dead stumps and roots of the Southern pine called "fat lighter," "liter," or "lighter-wood." Many campers use short, thick candles and commercial fire starters as tinder.

Never use gasoline or other flammable material as a fire starter. More than one backcountry traveler has gone to his reward early trying to start a quick fire with gasoline.

Once you have a good supply of tinder, place it in the round portion of the keyhole fire ring. Next, get a generous supply of small sticks and twigs. Place these small sticks over the tinder and slowly add slightly larger sticks until you have a fire that can ignite the larger wood. Remember not to rush the fire. If you place the heavier wood on too soon, you will smother the fire.

When traveling in snow country, the same fire-building principles will apply; however, the use of the keyhole rock ring may not be possible. In order to get a fire going in the snow, pick a site sheltered from the wind and with no overhanging branches, which might dump snow on your fire or catch fire. If the snow is not deep, dig down to the bare earth before building a fire. If you are in deep snow, pack the snow with your boots at the fire site. Make a platform of two-inch green sticks on which to build the fire. This will slow down the sinking of your fire into the snow.

Safety with a campfire cannot be overemphasized. Every year many camps are burned to the ground and forest fires are started by campfires left unattended. Last year some friends of mine were on a deer hunt in Alabama. They chose a good site for a campfire and were careful with it when they were around. One morning they were in such a hurry to get into the woods that they left their breakfast fire smoldering when they went hunting. Later, a strong wind came up and blew hot sparks onto their tent. The tent caught fire and destroyed several hundred dollars' worth of equipment. It was only luck that prevented a major forest fire.

Never leave a fire or even hot coals unattended. It is also a good precaution to keep a bucket of water and shovel handy in the event a campfire does get out of control.

When you are ready to break camp and move on, do the following:

1. Pick up all trash of any kind to pack out with you.
2. If possible, put your fire out several hours before you leave.
3. Scatter the rocks, firewood, dead charcoal, etc.

4. Replace the ground cover as it was before you arrived.

5. Leave the site as though no one had been there.

THE FIREPLACE FIRE

As I stated in the introduction, this book is intended for home and cabin use as well as for remote camp use. For this reason, I will discuss how to build a fire in the fireplace. Many fireplace owners do not realize that up until the 1800s most of the home cooking in North America was done in the fireplace. If necessary, fireplaces could be sources of cooking again. The same cooking techniques that apply to the campfire apply to the fireplace. The Dutch oven got its start in home fireplaces and is being used in some home fireplaces now as a fun change-of-pace method of cooking. Reflector ovens also work well in conjunction with a fireplace. My neighbors love to come into my den when a loaf of sourdough bread is baking in my reflector oven in front of the fireplace. Aluminum foil cooking and general campfire cooking can convert your fireplace into a mini-kitchen if there is a sudden power or gas supply failure.

According to the latest research from the U.S. Forest Service, the best way to build a fire in your fireplace starts by placing two logs on the iron grate or fire basket, and laying the tinder between them. Dry scrap paper may be more readily available than the classical tinder such as hemlock twigs and cedar or birch bark. Next, add a small handful of twigs or split softwood kindling, then place more dry logs over this base. A tepee formation of kindling and small branch wood will ease your fire through early combustion stages until the logs are aglow. Place these logs close—the narrow air spaces between them promote better drafts. The heat reflected between adjacent surfaces aids in raising and maintaining combustion temperatures.

Four logs generally make a satisfactory fire. Naturally, larger hardwood logs will burn longer. Adjust the logs and maintain the flames by pushing the ends into the flame from time to time. Add kindling and new logs as needed to rekindle a dying glow. Rake coals toward the front of the grate before adding new logs. Add new logs at the rear of the fireplace; there they will reflect light and heat into the room.

Ashes should only accumulate for an inch or two at the bottom of the grate. The ashes under the grate are important for they form a bed for the glowing coals that drop through the grate, concentrate heat, and direct drafts of air up to the base of the fire. Covering the burning logs with these excess ashes can check a flaming fire. A fire "banked" with ashes in this way will hold glowing coals for eight to ten hours, making it easier to rekindle the flames.

For safety, make sure your room is well ventilated, your damper is open, and flue unplugged before lighting the fire. Poor ventilation will cause the fireplace to smoke. Avoid burning wet or green wood. Place a screen in front of the grate to catch any sparks that fly. Keep a fire extinguisher handy and keep other combustibles at a distance. Never use flammable liquids indoors to light a fire.

Normally dry wood burned with abundant oxygen produces carbon dioxide, water, and a small amount of residual ash—all of which may be easily recycled by green plants. Burning green or wet wood results in increased production of wood tars and several associated smoke products. These tars and the wood extracts may condense in the chimney flue and could result in a chimney fire if ignited. Unseasoned wood coupled with poor ventilation or an obstructed chimney leads to all sorts of irritation. Eye, nose, and mucous membranes are first to react to smoke even at nontoxic levels. Tempers are next if smoking persists.

Some modern homes, especially those with electric heating, are constructed to be so airtight that an air vent may have to be installed to ventilate the fireplace. When wood or charcoal is burned without sufficient oxygen, some carbon monoxide will be released.

Franklin stoves or glass fireplace doors offer a possible means of regulating drafts and may reduce the amount of smoke that escapes into the room. If, however, the reason for poor fireplace performance is faulty construction, the only safe solution is proper rebuilding.

Some materials that should never be burned in a fire include plastics, poison ivy twigs and stems, and chemically treated woods such as discarded utility poles and railroad ties. Many individuals are extremely sensitive to small amounts of these smoke-associated chemicals.

When softwoods are used in fire building, brief, vigorous fires result without a bed of long-lasting coals. When any unburned fuels have been pushed to the rear of the grate and the fireplace opening is covered with a fine mesh screen, a softwood fire can be presumed safe enough to be left unattended.

Some resinous woods are best used as stove woods or only with caution in the fireplace. Hemlock, larch, spruce, and juniper all contain moisture pockets in the wood. Upon heating, trapped gases and water vapor build pressure in these pockets and pop with great vigor. This popping is another reason for reducing moisture content as much as possible before burning any firewood.

Firewood can be cut in many national and state forests for free or with low-cost permits. Once you have gathered the tinder and kindling and have selected the logs to practice your skills at fire building, enjoy the warmth and beauty of your fireplace all winter long.

KEEPING THE COOK KIT CLEAN

There are two schools of thought on the best way to treat aluminum cookware used over open fires. The first involves coating the shiny cookware's outer surface with a paste made from soap and water. The soot from the fire gets on this coating and washes off easily leaving shiny cookware. Caution should be used with this method so that the soap does not get into the inside of the pot or pan. If it does, it can cause stomach upset.

The second method is to let the cookware blacken over the fire to collect heat faster and thereby cook faster.

You be the judge. I have tried both ways and they both work.

CUTTING TOOLS

There are several tools for cutting firewood at home, in base camps, and in remote wilderness camps.

For base camps and home use I like a bow saw with a thirty-inch blade. This saw is compact and one person can handle it without any trouble. Covering it with a split, discarded section of garden hose can protect the blade.

Many backpackers have gone to the quarter-ounce twisted-toothed wire saw. It has finger rings at each end and does an adequate job if you do not need very much wood.

Last year I packed into the mountains of northern New Mexico with an old-timer who used a wooden handled jack saw that folded like a pocketknife. It was a little slow cutting, but it worked well on wood and meat.

Perhaps the most popular saw around homes and some base camps is the chain saw. While I dislike their noise, they do a most efficient job of providing a generous supply of firewood in a hurry. Since many people are not familiar with these saws, here are some dangers and safety rules that everyone using a chain saw should know:

- Chain saw hazards result from contact with the moving chain during "kickback," accidental acceleration, and touching hot muffler surfaces with skin or clothing.
- Avoid cutting above shoulder height. You can lose control on completion of the cut and the saw can swing into your body.
- Falling trees can be a hazard to the operator who does not plan direction of the fall or a safe retreat.
- Wear protective footwear, safety clothing, and ear and eye protection.

Before operating a chain saw, follow this checklist:

1. Clear area of branches, sticks, and other objects, which could be thrown by the chain.
2. Refuel before starting the saw and clean up spills immediately.
3. Start the saw at least ten feet from where it was fueled.

During operation:

4. Keep a firm hold with both hands on saw handles; maintain good balance.
5. Keep hands and feet clear of chain blade at all times, and keep body out of line of cut.
6. Keep bystanders away from the work area.
7. Never operate in closed, unventilated areas.
8. Keep the chain well oiled while cutting.
9. Wear safety glasses and ear protection.

For safety maintenance, the operator should check frequently for leaking fuel lines, proper chain tension, and loose fasteners.

As lightweight chain saws become less expensive and available at more stores throughout the country, outdoorsmen are finding increasing numbers of uses for the powerful, portable tools—cutting browse for deer, building game bird blinds, or constructing rustic camp furniture. Many hunting lodges and cabins have been con-structed with a chain saw serving as the builder's only power tool.

SOME CAMPFIRE WOODS EVALUATED

Species	Relative Amount of Heat	Easy to Burn?	Easy to Split?	Heavy Smoke?	Comments
Ash	High	Yes	Yes	No	Excellent
Beech	High	Yes	Yes	No	Excellent
Cherry	Medium	Yes	Yes	No	Good
Dogwood	High	Yes	Yes	No	Excellent
Elm	Medium	Moderate	No	Moderate	Fair
Gum	Medium	Moderate	No	Moderate	Fair
Hickory	High	Yes	Yes	No	Excellent
Maple (hard)	High	Yes	Yes	No	Excellent
Maple (soft)	Medium	Yes	Yes	No	Good
Oak (mixed)	High	Yes	Yes	No	Excellent
Pecan	High	Yes	Yes	No	Excellent
Southern Yellow Pine	High	Yes	Yes	Yes	Good
White Pine	Low	Moderate	Yes	Moderate	Fair*
Sycamore	Medium	Moderate	No	Moderate	Fair
Yellow Poplar	Low	Yes	Yes	Moderate	Fair*

*Good kindling.

CHAPTER

Cooking Without Utensils

N ow that we have modern lightweight foods that are quick
and easy to prepare, it seems strange to hear someone discuss cooking without utensils, better known as primitive
cooking. However, the need arises from time to time for one to recall these almost forgotten skills. During my own outdoor career,
aside from teaching survival courses or attending mountain man
rendezvous, I have sometimes found myself in a situation that required primitive cooking skills. I was once lost for three days on a
deer hunt and found myself cooking chipmunks over hot coals on a
hickory stick. On another occasion, a canoeing mishap left me
walking in a strange land for several days. Not having any equipment left me cooking with what I could find. For these and other
reasons I include this chapter.

The primitive man knew more about fires than most modern
people. He knew that the best heat came from hot coals and not
from leaping flames. The first step when cooking without utensils is
to build a fire in a pit no larger than twenty to thirty inches in diameter and approximately ten inches deep. Line the bottom of the pit
with rocks. Make sure the rocks do not come from a streambed,
since these may explode when heated. Allow the fire to burn until
you have a hot bed of coals. You are now ready to cook.

Perhaps the easiest method of primitive cooking is the use of a
spit. You may recall seeing some tough character on television or in
a cowboy movie cooking a rabbit over the campfire on a stick. That
is one form of spit cooking. Another way is to cut two Y-shaped
sticks and stick them into the ground on either side of the fire pit.
They should be the same height above the ground, some fourteen
to sixteen inches above the coals. Next, impale the food on a hori-

zontal spit and rest it in the forks of the upright sticks. Rotate the spit every ten to fifteen minutes, one-quarter turn, to cook the food evenly. For any type of spit cooking, always use a hardwood green stick for the spit. A softwood spit will leave a resinous taste.

To cook a steak or similar cut of meat, use a spit that is forked at the end. Stick the fork into the meat from the narrow side. This will permit you to turn the meat over without having it slip.

The famous gypsy spit is an efficient way to cook large pieces of meat. Construct a tripod over the pit fire. Each leg of the tripod should be about four feet long. Wrap a piece of wire tightly around the meat. Tie a doubled rope at the apex of the tripod and let it hang down to within twenty inches of the coals. Attach the wire around the meat to the rope. Twist the rope so it will unwind and rewind itself. The meat should be approximately ten inches above the coals. The spinning meat will cook evenly within an hour.

Bread can be cooked on a spit as well. Simply wrapping it in a coil around a stick and holding it over the fire will cook bannock and other breads. By slowly turning the stick, you can cook the bread evenly.

Fish are often difficult to cook on a spit. The best way to cook fish is to weave a grill out of the green branches of a hardwood tree. Weave long branches over and under each other at right angles; with some practice you will find this to be an easy chore. The bending branches keep enough tension to remain in place. Sometimes it is necessary to tie the corners to keep the grill together. The grill should be rested on stones about ten inches above the coals for cooking. Obviously the grill will soon dry out, and it will be necessary to construct a new one.

My brother has developed a method of smoking meat that works well in base camps. He calls it smoke-hole cooking and declares that a base camp without a smoke hole is like a man who has never owned a good bird dog—once he gets one he cannot understand how he managed without it. The smoke hole offers a method of cooking with smoke that can make meat taste better than anything you have ever eaten.

Dig a hole (fire pit) about eighteen inches square and from it dig a shallow smoke trench six inches square. Cover the trench with flat rocks and bank it with dirt to keep the smoke from escaping. At the end of the trench, which should be four or five feet long, build

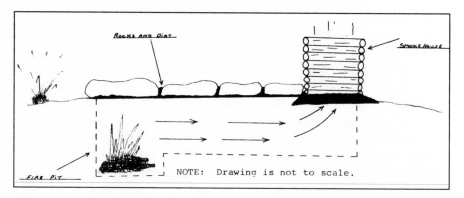

NOTE: Drawing is not to scale.

The smoke hole cooking technique.

the smokehouse by cutting and notching saplings and putting them together log-cabin fashion until three or four feet high.

Another method is to drive four saplings into the ground to form the corners and cover them with aluminum foil. Bank the bottom of the smokehouse with dirt so no smoke escapes. Loosely place a few strips of bark over the top of the smokehouse to serve as a lid.

Hang strips of meat inside.

Get your fire going well in the pit with dry hardwood, and then add some green hardwood (hickory or oak will do). After the green wood catches fire, cover the pit with a flat rock and bank it with dirt. Properly built, a good fire will last for hours because the smokehouse acts as an efficient chimney.

Before you try cooking with smoke, remember that it takes hours for most meat to get done. Venison jerky can be dried entirely in the smokehouse, but most meat needs to be half-cooked over an open fire before it is put into the smokehouse. Organ cuts of venison, such as the heart, liver, or tongue, should be thoroughly cooked before smoking.

With some practice you can learn to use this method of smoke cooking well enough to satisfy any palate.

A good method of cooking any kind of food without utensils is to construct a rock oven. First dig a hole approximately two feet deep and two or three feet square, depending on the amount of food to be cooked. Then select rocks (but not from a stream bed since these rocks explode when heated), green limbs approximately three inches in diameter, plenty of firewood, and grass or leaves for insulation.

Lay firewood in the hole. Place the green limbs across the hole. Pile the rocks onto the green limbs. Light the fire and keep it stoked. When the green limbs burn through and the rocks fall into the hole, the oven is ready to use.

Remove the rocks and ashes and clean any live fire from the hole. Line the bottom of the hole with hot rocks and place a thin layer of dirt over the rocks. Place grass, moss, or other insulating material on the dirt. Put in the food to be cooked, more insulating material, a thin layer of dirt, hot rocks, and cover over with remaining earth.

Small pieces of meat such as steak or chops cook in one and one-half to two hours. Large roasts take five to six hours.

Broiling is another way to prepare fish. A rock broiler may be made by placing a layer of small stones on top of hot hardwood coals and laying the fish on the top. Cooked in this manner, it is moist and delicious. Crabs and lobsters may also be placed on the stones and broiled.

Vegetables, fruits, and eggs may also be cooked on a rock broiler. The egg should be pierced in the small end and placed on the rocks with the large end down. Prop in place and turn often. It will cook in approximately ten minutes.

While I was working on the first edition of this book, I traveled into the headwater country of the Stikine River in British Columbia. Due to some unfortunate circumstances, I was stranded on a remote lake without food and cooking utensils. No one knew where I was and I wasn't sure how long I would have to make the best of my situation. I found that catching rainbow trout and grayling was very easy, so I turned to primitive cooking techniques in order to eat. It was several days before I signaled a bush plane in to get me. During that time, I enjoyed fish on hot rocks, fish on a stick, and woven stick fish.

CHAPTER 4

Cooking with Aluminum Foil

The morning had been one of the best squirrel hunts of the season. The December air was cold, all the leaves had dropped off the big hardwoods, and the little fox terrier had treed seven times before lunch.

This was an annual hunt for Buck Rivers and me. Each year before Christmas, we would take his fox terrier and squirrel hunt around the top of Tater Knob Mountain in North Alabama. It had become somewhat of a custom to eat lunch at Soapstone Spring on each of these hunts.

On this particular hunt we reached the spring around noon and got a fire going. Once I got warm I searched throughout my hunting vest and found to my dismay that my lunch sack was still in the car. Buck must have seen the forlorn look on my face. "Fergit ye lunch did ye?" he chuckled. "Dress out one of them squirrels and ye can eat with me."

Buck reached into an old army surplus bag, which doubled as a game bag and carrier of hunting needs, and pulled out a large potato, one carrot, a healthy onion, and a folded sheet of aluminum foil. Next, he made an envelope out of the foil. By the time I had the squirrel cleaned, he had the vegetables cut up into little squares and piled into the foil envelope. Buck then took the squirrel, cut it into quarters, and placed it in the envelope with the vegetables. His last step was to tightly fold the top of the envelope closed, and to toss it into the bed of coals.

As we sat reliving the morning's hunt, Buck occasionally turned the foil package over. Within thirty minutes, he fished the package out of the fire and presented me with one of the best trail lunches I have ever eaten. Rather than a soggy sandwich, we had a hot, nourishing meal with no pots to clean, and, perhaps best of all, we left no trash behind. Upon completion of the meal, Buck simply wadded the aluminum foil into a ball and tucked it into his bag. We were ready for the afternoon's hunt.

Cooking with aluminum foil is not a new trick. People have been using this unique method since aluminum foil was introduced in the mid-1940s. Many cooking experts say that cooking in aluminum foil is modern man's version of preparing food in leaves and clay.

I fondly recall my reasons for enjoying aluminum foil cooking back when I was a member of Boy Scout Troop 70 in the early 1950s. (In fact, I still like to cook with aluminum foil for the same reasons.) It gives you more time to enjoy the outdoors since it reduces the time necessary for cleaning pots and pans. Cooking with aluminum foil can cut down on the number of pans you take with you. Also, you can cook almost anything in it including meats, fruits, and vegetables. Properly wrapped and sealed, each foil bundle becomes a pressure cooker. The trapped steam retains flavor and prevents scorching. When scorching occurs it is usually because steam is permitted to escape through a tear in the foil or a loosely sealed wrapping.

Trying to explain to someone how long to cook an aluminum foil dish is almost impossible. By far, the best teacher is experience. In foil cooking, timing is not as critical as in other forms of cooking, so you can learn without spoiling the meal.

When cooking in foil be sure to place the food on the shiny side of the foil. Tests have proven that the shiny side of the foil reflects more radiant heat than it absorbs.

There is some disagreement about which works best—heavy duty or lightweight foil. Those who use the heavy-duty foil say it is more desirable because of its additional strength. Those who use the lightweight foil usually wrap their food in two to three layers. They give three reasons for using layers of lightweight foil: First, it is less likely to leak steam; second, when they remove the bundle from the fire they take off the outer wrap, thereby getting rid of the ashes; and third, layers are less likely to break or tear than the single wrap. Both methods seem to work fine, so you be the judge.

A forked stick and aluminum foil can be made into a skillet. *Photo courtesy of Reynolds Metal Company.*

The only equipment you will need for aluminum foil cooking is a shovel for moving coals around, a strong stick to use with the shovel for turning and moving the foil bundles, and a pair of gloves for handling the bundles and peeling the aluminum foil.

Many people make a common mistake when cooking with aluminum foil. They throw their foil-wrapped food into a hot fire and consequently the food is burned. The best cooking fire to use is one that has burned down to a two-inch bed of coals. Rake away enough hot coals to expose the ground. Place your foil bundle on the exposed ground and rake the hot coals over the bundle until it is covered. Keep hot coals on the bundle, especially when you have turned it over. Charcoal briquettes can also be used.

Here are some examples of recipes you can make with this aluminum-foil cooking method.

BREAKFAST APPLES

Core large baking apples and peel skin from upper part. Place on squares of aluminum foil. Fill centers with orange marmalade, top with chopped walnuts, and sprinkle with lemon juice to keep cut surface from discoloring. Wrap in foil, twisting at top to close. Place in coals and cook about 45 minutes. Test for doneness by piercing with fork through foil.

FOIL FISH

Spread 1 teaspoon of margarine in the center of a large sheet of aluminum foil. Place 2 small trout or bluegill on the buttered foil. Next, butter the fish and season with salt and pepper to taste. On top of the fish slice 1 small potato and onion. Cover with catsup. Seal in the foil and place in hot coals. Allow 10 minutes per side. Serves 2.

BEAN DELIGHT

Divide a 16-oz. can of pork and beans into 4 portions on 4 squares (9″ X 9″) of aluminum foil. Add crosscut sections of 4 frankfurters to each. Top with chopped onion, ¼ teaspoon Worcestershire sauce, 1 teaspoon of catsup, and a dash of pepper. Bring up foil and seal tightly. Cook in coals for 10 minutes. Serves 4.

HOBO STEW

Cut tender beef into 1-inch cubes. Place sufficient meat cubes for an individual serving in center of sheet of aluminum foil. Add 1 small ripe tomato, green pepper rings, 1 sliced carrot, 1 medium onion, 1 potato (quartered) to each packet. Season with salt, pepper, and a pinch of oregano. Add a pat of butter or margarine to each. Seal foil with a double fold to make a tight package. Cook in coals approximately 45 minutes.

CAMP SHRIMP

Peel and de-vein 2 lbs. of large raw shrimp (fresh or frozen). Cream ½ cup butter or margarine and add 1 large garlic clove (minced), 1 teaspoon Worcestershire sauce, ½ teaspoon salt, ¼ teaspoon freshly ground coarse pepper (black), and ½ cup minced parsley. Mix well. Tear off six 9-inch lengths of 18-inch wide aluminum foil. Fold each sheet in half to form a 9-inch, double-thickness square. Divide shrimp equally among the foil squares and top shrimp with butter mixture. Bring foil up around shrimp and twist tightly to seal. Place foil packets directly on hot coals. Barbecue 5 minutes. Makes 6 generous servings.

BAKED POTATOES

Scrub several large baking potatoes and tightly wrap them individually in aluminum foil. Place them on coals around the edge of the fire. Bake about 45 minutes or until done. To test for doneness, insert fork through the foil. Even the skins will be edible and delicious. You can use this same procedure to bake sweet potatoes.

CORN-ON-THE-COB

Remove husks and silks. Brush corn with melted butter or margarine and wrap tightly in foil. Place on top of coals. Foil seals in that fresh corn flavor and aroma. Turn occasionally. Roasts in about 20 minutes.

Banana Dessert

Take a banana (leaving the peel on), split it down the middle, and fill the split with caramel candy. Wrap the banana with aluminum foil and toss onto a bed of hot coals. Remove in 10 minutes when the candy has melted into the hot banana.

Aluminum foil not only makes a good food wrap for campfire cooking, but it also is handy for making cooking utensils. Many backcountry travelers include foil in their survival kits. It can be used for making a water container, frying pan, reflector oven, or skillet. Foil can also be used as an emergency signaling device; the reflective surface can be seen a long way on a bright day.

Be sure to bring out of the backcountry all the aluminum foil you took in. At one time it was a common practice to bury foil, but it was found to last as long as aluminum beer cans, and bears, raccoons, and other critters dug it up. Bring your aluminum foil and other trash home and dispose of it properly. You and future generations will be glad you did.

The Versatile Dutch Oven

My work was cut out for me. It was the third day of a week-long deer hunt in Georgia and it was my day to be camp cook. That is usually not a difficult task, but when you are cooking for several 200-plus-pounders, it becomes a chore! These overgrown hunters eat enormous amounts of food after a full day of deer hunting.

With this background information you can imagine their surprised looks when they walked into our tent camp late that afternoon to see me cooking in a black pot buried under coals from our campfire. What these modern camper-hunters were witnessing was the use of America's first cook kit—the cast iron Dutch oven. It was not until I took a shovel, removed the hot coals from the top of the Dutch oven, and removed the lid that they learned the magic in that black pot had produced a squirrel Brunswick stew.

The Dutch oven has been used since America's frontier was along the Atlantic seaboard. In those early days, most cooking was done outdoors, in a fireplace, or in a lean-to behind the cabin. The settlers made a large cast iron pot, with a flat lid, that could be placed directly into the coals of an open fire. Heat was distributed evenly throughout the pot since it was constructed of heavy cast iron. Early cooks learned that by heaping hot coals onto the flat lid, this newly designed pot could be used for baking, and roasting was improved.

It is said that skilled craftsman Paul Revere perfected the final design of the Dutch oven. This design is still used today.

Once the cast iron pot became popular, New England manufacturers produced it in large numbers. It was not uncommon for

Dutch traders to stop by to purchase large quantities of the pot for trading with the Indians; thus, the pot became known as the "Dutch" oven.

As the westward movement crossed the Appalachian Mountains and traveled down the Ohio River, so did the Dutch oven. Almost all early explorers, mountain men, military expeditions, and settlers depended upon the Kentucky rifle and the Dutch oven. The rifle supplied the game and the Dutch oven transformed the game into a meal. History has recorded that one of the most valued pieces of equipment carried on the Lewis and Clark expedition was a large-sized Dutch oven.

The Dutch oven has been used through the years without improvement upon its cooking qualities or design. Only one change has been made in modern history: aluminum models can now be purchased. But cast iron still cooks best if weight is not a problem.

Today, the true Dutch oven can only be purchased in such places as hardware stores, Boy Scout supply dealers, and a few outdoor equipment mail-order houses; or they may be purchased from the manufacturer (see suppliers list in the back of this book).

When buying a Dutch oven, make sure you are getting the real thing. It is made of heavy cast iron, with a flat bottom sitting on three short legs protruding about two inches. It will have a strong wire bail. The lid is made of the same heavy cast iron and will have a small handle in the center. The rim of the lid is flanged so that hot coals will stay on the lid while cooking. You can get the Dutch oven in several sizes, usually from eight inches to sixteen inches in diameter, and from four to six inches deep. The twelve-inch diameter size is the most popular for family-sized cooking. The weight ranges from seven to thirty pounds for the large size. One word of caution: many modern-day flat-bottomed pots are called Dutch ovens. Make sure you are getting the one described above, which is specifically designed for open-fire cooking.

When you get your new Dutch oven home the first step is to make sure the lid will seat well on the pot. If it does not, the remedy is simple. Smear valve-grinding compound on the rim of the pot and the edge of the lid, and then rotate the lid until you have a good tight fit.

The real campfire Dutch oven is the one on the right, with the legs.

After getting the lid to seat properly, give the Dutch oven a good cleaning with hot water and soap. Thoroughly scrub the pot and lid with a stiff bristle brush. This should be the only time your Dutch oven will be washed with soap. This washing process is necessary because manufacturers coat new Dutch ovens with protective waxes or oils that must be washed off before the oven is used. Rinse the oven well and towel-dry it.

The next step to take is the most important one—breaking it in, often called "sweetening" it. Since all cast iron is porous, breaking it in is essential if the Dutch oven is to perform at its best. There are many ways to break a Dutch oven in, but the one most often used is to nearly fill it with good cooking oil and have a fish fry, keeping the oil hot until it works out to the exterior. Be sure the underside of the lid gets the same oil treatment.

Another method of sweetening the oven is to smear all inside surfaces of the pot and lid with a heavy coat of cooking oil or grease. Next, put them into your home oven with the temperature set on 350°F. Bake the Dutch oven for an hour, using a brush every fifteen minutes to coat it with more oil or grease. This can be a smoky job—you will want to open a few windows.

The Dutch oven lid may be used for frying.

Once the sweetening process is completed the Dutch oven should never again be washed with soapy water. Surprisingly, the Dutch oven will usually wipe clean without any strong detergents or scrubbing. With reasonable care and use, the Dutch oven will last a lifetime and get "sweeter" each time it is used.

Now that the Dutch oven is properly sweetened, it is ready for use. The most versatile piece of cooking gear available, it can be used for deep fat frying, shallow frying, roasting, baking, boiling, or stewing. You can cook with either dry heat or moist heat. With the Dutch oven you are limited only by your imagination.

For baking, I have found that a round cake rack placed in the bottom of the oven does an excellent job, especially with bread-stuffs and pies. It keeps food from sticking to the bottom and makes cleaning up easier. I use charcoal briquettes for baking in my Dutch oven. When the proper number of briquettes is used for a particular size of Dutch oven, the results are as good as with coals from a wood fire.

Here are the formulas I have worked out:

NUMBER OF BRIQUETTES

Oven Size	Top	Bottom
8"	8	6
10"	15	13
12"	20	15
14"	25	20
16"	30	25

I have found the best way to place the briquettes is to leave a two-inch square between them, forming a checkerboard pattern. Since charcoal briquettes give off a great deal of heat, you will want to check the food periodically.

If you are using more than one Dutch oven try "stack cooking" to save on charcoal briquettes or to give you more room around the campfire. After you have the first Dutch oven heating properly, set the second on top of the first and add hot briquettes or coals to its lid. I have seen outfitters stack as many as five Dutch ovens and serve campfuls of hungry hunters quickly as a result. I have settled on a fourteen-inch oven for my main course with a smaller ten-inch oven sitting on top of it baking bread at the same time.

It is possible to bake two dishes in the Dutch oven at once if they require about the same amount of cooking time. Simply place each foodstuff in a separate pan and place the pans in the oven on the cake rack.

I have been on many extended canoe trips where the Dutch oven was my entire cook kit. During one of these trips, I learned that the Dutch oven lid, when turned upside down and placed on a small bed of hot coals, makes an excellent frying pan. If you are using charcoal briquettes you can turn the pot upside down, place eight to ten briquettes on the bottom of the pot, and then set the lid upside down on the pot legs and fry away. It also serves as a superb camp griddle.

In order to handle the hot ovens and to move hot coals I carry three (and what I consider essential) tools with my Dutch ovens. The first is a short-handled army surplus shovel used for spreading coals, placing coals on the lid, and digging pits for cooking. The second tool is a short fireplace poker that I have bent into a hook at

Two dishes baking at once—called stack cooking.

the bottom. This poker allows me to move a hot oven, to lift a hot lid when checking food, and to move charcoal briquettes around for proper spacing. The third tool is a whiskbroom that I use to sweep ashes off the lid before looking inside the pot.

My two Dutch ovens have added to my home decor, too. Instead of storing the ovens with the rest of my camping gear in the garage, I placed them on either side of my den fireplace. My friends constantly ask me where I got those priceless antiques. I discovered that my Dutch ovens work just as well in my home fireplace as they do in a campfire—an added plus during a power failure and a fun way to save energy. The Dutch oven can also be used with a wood-burning stove. Simply set it on top of or to one side of the stove where the heat is not too intense and cook away.

By following the cooking directions and recipes given in this chapter, you can use your Dutch ovens as a home survival kit during an energy crisis, or they can be used as a change of pace when cooking for friends. I like to cook an entire meal in Dutch ovens in my den fireplace. My friends are amazed at my pioneer skills and they enjoy the "different" way of cooking. If we were to have a total economic or energy breakdown, your Dutch ovens could turn your fireplace into a workable cooking unit.

One of the best ways the Dutch oven can serve you in camp is by cooking slowly, all day, unattended, while you are out hunting, fishing, hiking, or whatever. When you get back to camp tired and starving, dinner is ready. Here is the slow-cooking method I learned from an old camp cook in the Rio Grande National Forest of Colorado when I was guiding elk hunters.

"Grump," as he was fondly called, would set his Dutch oven next to the campfire to preheat while he prepared breakfast for the hunters. While they ate breakfast he would prepare the ingredients for a stew. Next, Grump would dig a hole near the campfire some two feet deep and eighteen inches in diameter. Into the bottom of the hole, he would put two or three shovelfuls of glowing red coals from the campfire. Then, he would place the stew ingredients into the warm Dutch oven, replace the lid, and lower it into the hole of coals. He would then shovel in enough hot coals to cover the oven and loosely shovel an inch of dirt on top of the coals for insulation, being careful not to smother them. Throughout the day the stew would simmer, but not burn, and that night's dinner was ready whenever the hunters returned.

I have used this "dirt hole" method of cooking many times and it worked without failure each time. This cooking method works especially well in a camp where a cook is not available throughout the day.

Recipes for Dutch-oven cooking are essentially the same as recipes for cooking on your stove at home. The main difference is the source of heat. Some interesting special recipes have come about due to people's interest in Dutch-oven cooking; I think you will find these few samples of interest.

The Brunswick stew recipe I use is over 200 years old. It has been said that such notables as Patrick Henry and Alexander Hamilton ate this celebrated stew at Cold Spring Club and City Tavern in Philadelphia. Dr. Creed Haskins cooked the first stew at Brunswick, Virginia, and it became traditional at cockfights, rifle matches, and political rallies.

Brunswick Stew

2 squirrels	*1½ teaspoon salt*
2 quarts boiling water	*½ teaspoon pepper*
2 potatoes	*2 cups tomatoes*
1 onion	*1½ teaspoons sugar*
1 cup corn	*¼ cup butter*
1 cup lima beans	

Put 2 squirrels, which have been cut into 6 pieces, into the boiling water in the Dutch oven along with the potatoes, onion, corn, lima beans, salt, and pepper; cover and simmer for 2 hours.

Add tomatoes and sugar and simmer for an additional hour.

Add the butter and simmer again for 30 minutes. Bring the stew to a boil and move it over to the edge of the fire to keep warm while you sneak out of camp for an hour of deer hunting before dark. Serves 4. (One large chicken cut into 6 pieces can be substituted for squirrels.)

The Dutch oven can bake any type of bread. Bannock or sourdough bread is especially good baked in the Dutch oven. See the chapters on these delicious breads for recipes.

When I was a small boy growing up on the side of Tater Knob Mountain in Alabama, I always looked forward to being asked to help my dad run his trap lines on the Flint River. It was on these adventures that my dad would fry up a Tater Knob Hoe Cake in his well-worn Dutch oven.

Tater Knob Hoecake

1 cup self-rising corn meal	*1 egg*
dash of salt	*enough water or buttermilk to make a paste*

Heat the Dutch oven over the coals of the campfire and add a small amount of cooking oil. When the oil gets hot, pour in the hoecake paste made from combining the ingredients above, letting it brown on the bottom before turning. A hot hoecake and a cup of strong black coffee make a good breakfast. Serves 2.

DUTCH OVEN BAKED FISH

Here is a simple way to bake fish. Flour several small fish. Salt to taste. Place in buttered Dutch oven and add ½ cup of tomato juice. Cover lid and place in hot coals. Add hot coals to top of lid and bake for 30 minutes. Allow 2 fish per person.

DUTCH OVEN BEANS

1 2-lb. can pork and beans
4 thick slices of bacon
Liquid Smoke to taste

½ cup brown sugar
¼ cup mustard
¼ cup catsup

Mix beans thoroughly with brown sugar, mustard, catsup, and Liquid Smoke. Put into Dutch oven and place bacon on top of beans. Cover and bury in coals at least 1 hour. The oven can stay in the coals for a long period without burning. Serves 6. A fast way to have a good baked bean dish at home or at camp.

DUTCH OVEN APPLE SURPRISE

Wash and core 8 apples. Place raisins, 1 teaspoon butter, ½ teaspoon cinnamon, and 1 teaspoon sugar into the holes. Place apples on a greased pie tin with enough water to cover bottom. Place tin in Dutch oven on cake rack to prevent scorching. Cover, place oven in hot coals, and cover lid with hot coals. Bake for 30 minutes. Serves 8.

SHERRIED QUAIL

4 whole quail
salt to taste
1 cup sherry wine

freshly ground pepper to taste
½ cup butter or margarine

Thoroughly clean each bird; season with salt and pepper. In Dutch oven over hot coals, brown birds evenly on all sides in butter. Pour wine over them. Cover and simmer slowly for 45 minutes to 1 hour, or until tender. Serves 2 to 4.

BAKED RATTLESNAKE

1 rattlesnake (or chicken)
1 can cream sauce
1 jar sliced mushrooms
2 limes, sliced thinly

1 teaspoon basil
1 teaspoon white pepper
1 teaspoon rosemary

Skin the snake, dress, and wash in cold water. Cut into 3-inch sections and place into a Dutch oven. Cover with cream sauce. Add mushrooms, limes, basil, pepper, and rosemary. Cover and place on hot coals adding coals on lid. Bake for ½ hour or until done. Serves 4.

VENISON STEW

2 cloves garlic
1 onion, sliced
3 tablespoons shortening
2 lbs. venison (or beef)
1 can tomato sauce
1 cup water

4 green peppers, chopped
3 potatoes, quartered
6 carrots, halved
2 bay leaves
6 medium onions
salt and pepper to taste

Fry sliced onion and garlic in shortening in Dutch oven. Add the meat and brown. Cover with tomato sauce and 1 cup water. Remove garlic; add carrots, pepper, potatoes, and whole onions. Add seasonings and additional water if necessary, then cook approximately 1 hour or until vegetables are tender. Add hot coals to top of the lid as well. Serves 6.

DUTCH OVEN VENISON

6 lbs. venison or beef roast
salt to taste
pepper to taste
meat tenderizer

hot water
dry onion soup mix
Worcestershire sauce
cold water

Put salt, pepper, and meat tenderizer on a 6-lb. venison or beef roast. Make a thick paste with hot water and dry onion soup mix and paint it over the entire roast. Sprinkle Worcestershire sauce over the roast. Add 1 cup of cold water to the Dutch oven, place roast into the oven, and cover. Place in hot coals, adding hot coals to the lid for approximately 4 to 5 hours. This dish can be cooked by using the "dirt hole" method discussed earlier. Serves 12.

These are but a few of the many ways you can cook with the versatile Dutch oven. With a little experience you can cook anything with a Dutch oven that you can cook on an electric or gas range. The major difference is that the Dutch oven uses little energy and can be used in the most remote places people can reach.

Its only limitation is its weight; most Dutch ovens are too heavy for backpacking.

CHAPTER *6*

Reflector-Oven Baking

Perhaps no other cooking technique is disappearing from the backcountry scene faster than reflector oven cooking. This highly efficient oven, handed down from early pioneer days, has contributed much to wilderness camps throughout North America. It has also been used in many homes and cabins, in conjunction with a fireplace or wood stove, to produce excellent meals. Tasty breads, pies, cakes, biscuits, puddings, roasted meat and fish, and casseroles can be cooked in this simple oven. Any foods that can be cooked in the home oven can be baked in the reflector oven.

In fact, I use my reflector oven in my den fireplace to bake breads, cookies, pies, and other delectables. It has become a favorite gathering place for close friends during cold evenings. The aroma of the baking goodies and the quaint way I bake had led many of my friends to purchase reflector ovens to add baking to the tasks of their fireplaces.

I was once on a remote float trip where the camp cook surprised everyone by serving hot fresh baked pizza one evening. He had used a reflector oven for this streamside Italian delight.

I am not sure why this art form of cooking is disappearing. Perhaps it is a backcountry skill that is just being overlooked, or perhaps the fast, freeze-dried foods have overshadowed this old wilderness luxury. Regardless of the reason, I can only find a couple of sources from which to purchase a reflector oven (see suppliers list in the back of this book). However, the energy situation may cause a revival of interest in this method of cooking, since it can be used in the home fireplace just as easily as on the Stikine River in Northern British Columbia.

A campfire and the reflector oven go hand-in-hand.

In order to learn how to use a reflector oven one must first understand the principle by which it works. The reflector oven is made from polished aluminum or polished sheet metal. It is constructed so that dry heat from a nearby fire is reflected from the walls of the oven around the food. The secret of even cooking with the oven is to protect the shiny surfaces of the metal to create the most efficient heat reflection. These surfaces should be washed with soft wool pads and non-abrasive soap when they get dull from use. When not in use or when being transported, the oven should be carried in a soft cloth bag.

Most reflector ovens are constructed so that they can be folded into a neat package measuring a foot square by half an inch thick. Weighing a pound or more, they are not usually found in a backpacker camp but are excellent for base camps, canoe camps, or for emergency use at home.

A reflector oven can be made from aluminum foil. Simply take a roll of heavy-duty aluminum foil and tear off a twenty-four-inch sheet. Fold in half so that the shiny sides are together. Open fold out to form a forty-five-degree angle. Wrap around sticks to make the V ridge. Next, close the ends on each side of the V with more aluminum foil. Turn the V on its side with the opening toward the fire. With a little practice and imagination you can make a very efficient reflector oven from aluminum foil.

The optimum fire for reflector-oven cooking is one that has some hot flames. The best results come from a fire that has a backlog or sheet of aluminum foil placed upright across the fire from the reflector oven. This reflects the heat into the oven, which should be only twelve inches from the flames. As with any type of open-fire cooking, experience will soon teach you how to regulate the heat in the oven by moving it closer to or farther from the fire. Building the fire up or letting it burn down can also adjust heat. Two reflector ovens can be best used when they are placed across the fire from each other so that they are facing each other. This way they can reflect heat into each other.

Diane Thomas, wilderness cooking expert and author of *Roughing It Easy,* states that it is possible to learn to guess the temperature in a reflector oven with reasonable accuracy by holding your hand just in front of the oven. If you can hold it there for only one or two seconds, the temperature is near 500°F If you can hold it there for three to four seconds, 400°F; six seconds, 300°F; and seven to ten seconds, 200°F.

When cooking with a reflector oven, keep an eye on the food to be sure it is cooking properly. Turn the food every few minutes to make sure it is cooking evenly.

One of the joys of reflector-oven cooking is that you do not have to be choosy about the wood you use on the fire; since the food is not cooked over the flames it will not be affected by the use of pine or other softwoods.

When cooking with a reflector oven, you can enjoy watching the food bake while you sit around the campfire or around your home fireplace. Here are some recipes to try in your reflector oven.

CINNAMON TOAST

Toast bread slices in a reflector oven until golden brown. While hot, spread with margarine. Sprinkle a mixture of 1 part cinnamon and 4 parts sugar on melted margarine.

CAMPFIRE MEAT LOAF

½ cup dry bread crumbs	*¼ cup grated onion*
1 cup milk	*1 teaspoon salt*
1½ lbs. ground beef	*½ teaspoon sage*
2 beaten eggs	*dash of pepper*

Soak bread crumbs in milk; add meat, eggs, onion, and seasonings; mix well. Form into individual loaves or place into greased muffin pans. Cover with catsup or sauce of your choice.

Bake in moderate oven (350°F) for 45 minutes to 1 hour. Makes 8 servings. Note: All pans must be greased.

CHERRY CAKE

Use an 8″ × 8″ pan or, if recipe is doubled, use an 11″ or 13″ × 9″ pan or baking dish.

Pour 1 can cherry pie filling into bottom of pan.

Sprinkle 1 box of single-layer white cake mix (dry) over the cherry pie filling.

Melt 1 stick or ½ cup butter or margarine and pour over white cake mix in pan.

Sprinkle ½ cup crushed nuts (walnuts, pecans) on top and bake at 350°F for 1 hour. Top will be brown and bubbly when done. Delicious served with vanilla ice cream. Serves 6.

ROASTED QUAIL WITH MUSHROOMS

4 quail, cleaned (or hens)　　*juice of half lemon*
4 slices bacon　　*½ cup hot water*
1 tablespoon butter or　　*1 3-oz. can broiled*
　margarine　　　*mushrooms, drained*

Wipe quail inside and out. Bind each bird with a slice of bacon. Put birds into a buttered pan and roast at 350°F basting occasionally, for about 30 minutes, or until tender. Remove birds and add butter or margarine, water, and lemon juice to drippings in pan, stirring to make a gravy. Add mushrooms. Serve the birds on toast with gravy poured over them. Serves 4.

BAKED FISH

Any large fish—trout, carp, buffalo fish, or catfish—can be baked for a delicious meal. Trout needs only to be gutted and cleaned; the scales are too small to be removed. Carp and buffalo fish should be "fleeced"; that is, the scales and the upper layer of skin should be removed with a sharp knife in such a way that the inner skin remains in place to hold the fish together during cooking. Allow 1 lb. per person.

After the fish is washed and dried, season it inside and out with salt and pepper. Place the fish into a pan and cover with strips of bacon held in place with toothpicks. Chicken broth, sliced onions, sliced carrot, and 2 tablespoons of dry sherry can be added to the fish. Cook in a moderate oven (about 350°F) until done.

WRAPPED DOGS

Using Bisquick made up according to package directions for biscuits, roll dough to ¼-inch thickness. Cut dough into strips. Split 12 wieners lengthwise to their centers. Place slices of cheese in the splits. Wrap cheese-filled wieners with dough strips. Place in 400°F reflector oven and bake until golden brown. Serves 4 to 6.

MEAT PIES

6¼-oz. canned ham, chicken, or
  turkey, drained and flaked
1 teaspoon poppy seed (opt.)
2 tablespoons margarine or
  butter, softened

2 cups Bisquick
⅔ cup evaporated milk
⅔ cup water
5 (4" × 4") Swiss cheese slices
2 teaspoons prepared mustard

Combine Bisquick and ⅔ cup or ½ small can evaporated milk mixed with equal part water. Stir until dough is soft and sticky. Then make 5 biscuits in 3½-inch-circle size and put in baking pan. Combine first 5 ingredients reserving about ⅓ cup. Spoon scant ¼ cup of meat mixture onto each flattened biscuit. Fold cheese slices into quarters; place over meat mixture, pressing slightly. Spoon remaining meat mixture over cheese. Press remaining 5 biscuits to 4-inch circles and slightly stretch each over meat mixture. Do not seal edges. Sprinkle tops with poppy seeds if desired. Bake at 375°F for 10 to 15 minutes or until golden brown. Serve warm. Makes 5 sandwiches.

BAKED SPAM

1 12-oz. can Spam
cloves
⅓ cup brown sugar

½ teaspoon vinegar
1 teaspoon prepared mustard
1 teaspoon water

Score and dot Spam with cloves. Bake 35 minutes basting with the brown sugar, vinegar, mustard, and water mixed into a sauce. If you like a lot of sauce on your meat you can double the ingredients for the sauce. Serves 4.

SWEET BALLS

1 cup molasses or honey   *2 cups flour*

Mix well. Form into 2-inch balls. Preheat reflector oven to about 350°F. Grease lightweight aluminum pan; press balls until they are ⅜ inch thick and place inside. Bake 12 minutes or until golden brown. They should be soft and chewy. Makes approximately 8 balls.

CHAPTER

7

The Sheepherder's Stove

As I look back over a lifetime spent in the outdoors, there are certain things that I have come to associate with adventure and excitement. The old sheepherder's stove is one of these things. When I hear someone speak of these little-known stoves I think of elk-hunting camps at the base of Chama Peak in Colorado, sandbar camps on the Middle Fork of the Salmon River in Idaho, and remote sheep-hunting camps in Alaska.

These sheet metal stoves have been in the backcountry longer than anyone can remember. Not long ago, I was penning a magazine article on the history of the sheepherder's stove, a tribute to this disappearing piece of American ingenuity. After a great deal of research, I came to the conclusion that no one knew much about its history. The stove has been in high-mountain hunting camps, line camps, trappers' cabins, and pack string camps in general since the frontier days.

Today, the basic sheepherder's stove is sold at several mail-order houses. One far-sighted individual took the basic design and improved it several years ago. P. D. Sims of Lovell, Wyoming, told me he was not satisfied with the sheepherder's stove. He felt that it was impracticable because the firebox was so small it had to be continually fired, and there was a lack of heat for baking. Sims wanted a stove that would heat a large tent or cabin, had space enough on top for a coffee pot plus two frying pans, an oven large enough to bake a turkey, and broke down for easy packing. After much experimenting, he came up with the Sims Sportsman. Now big game outfitters, the U.S. Forest Service, the Park Service, and many trappers and individual hunters use his stove.

The Sims wood-burning stove heats the tent and performs all functions of an efficient cooking stove.

I use the Sims stove and I must admit it is one of the best things that ever happened to a cold weather base camp where transportation by boat, pack mule, or vehicle is used. It is constructed of sheet metal and is fifteen inches high, thirteen inches wide, and twenty-two inches long when erected. It has a detachable shelf and an oven. Complete with shelf, oven, and stovepipe, the stove weighs thirty-six pounds.

As with any sheet metal stove, the Sims Stove will burn out someday; however, I know outfitters who have been using these stoves for sixteen hard years. The other suppliers listed in the back also make excellent stoves.

Regardless of which sheepherder's stove you like, they have all played an important role in exploring the backcountry of North America. I once spent a week with a Canadian trapper who warmed his entire cabin with one of these stoves. He told me that he bought it from an Indian who had been using it in his hunting camp. The old stove had had its stovepipe replaced, but other than that it was still turning out good meals and keeping a cabin warm.

Several years ago, my good friend Jake Neal, legendary packer and outfitter in La Jara, Colorado, sold his cabin on the Conejos River. Jake and his wife moved into a wall tent with a sheepherder's stove. He said it was as comfortable as his cabin.

There are many advantages to the sheepherder's stove. Fuel is available for gathering—you do not have to lug around combustible material. It heats a tent or cabin as well as it cooks, and ventilation is not a strong concern since most of the dangerous gases go up the stovepipe. And a standard sized stove will do the cooking for a party of half a dozen hungry campers.

While the sheepherder's stove has been used mostly in the West and the far North, many eastern campers are catching on to this old secret. This past hunting season I saw wall tents and sheepherder's stoves being used in deer hunting camps in Alabama, Virginia, and New York. Maybe this renewed interest will keep this old classic alive.

Using a sheepherder's stove in a tent requires some safety consciousness. Never set the stove closer than three feet to the tent wall. The high heat from the stove can set the fabric afire, specially an older tent that has been waterproofed with flammable wax. Always be sure to use a fireproof shield where the stovepipe goes through the tent roof or wall. These pipes get hot enough to set a tent on fire.

If the wall tent you use has a canvas or nylon floor, you will need to get a box containing three inches of sand or dirt on which to set your stove. This insulation can prevent burning a hole in the tent floor or burning the entire tent.

Be sure to buy a spark arrester to insert into the end of the stovepipe to prevent starting a forest fire. They may be purchased with your stove. If you cannot find one, a square of screen wire can do the job.

Learn to use the stove dampers so that you can adjust the amount of heat needed. It is easy to put in too much wood and suddenly have a roaring fire that is too hot for cooking and a downright danger in the tent. These stoves can do a lot with a little wood.

Be careful when moving around the stove, too. It is easy for someone unfamiliar with wood stoves to fall over against one or, as I saw early one morning in a survey camp, sit on it.

Before starting a fire in the stove, it is always best to place one inch of dirt or sand into the bottom of the stove. This seals the stove for a better draft, insulates against excessive heat setting something under the stove on fire, and prolongs the life of the stove.

Anytime you take the stove down be sure to knock or brush out the excess soot in the stovepipes. This makes packing much cleaner and prevents soot buildup in the pipes.

Cooking on the sheepherder's stove is like cooking on any stove. With a little experience you can master it easily. The top of the stove can be used as a griddle, and, if you get one without an oven, a reflector oven with the open side against the side of the stove will bake foods without any trouble.

STOVE TOP OVEN

Whether you are cooking on a sheepherder's stove or a gas fired camp stove, there are now ovens available that allow you to bake in camp as easily as if you were home. Two of these ovens are made

The Fox Hill Outfitters oven can be used on a sheepherder's stove or gas camp-stove to bake anything you can bake in the home oven. *Photo courtesy of the Fox Hill Corporation.*

by Fox Hill Corp. The Sportsman's Oven is sized for family cooking while the Outfitter's Oven allows you to bake for a camp full of hearty eaters. Both are compact, portable, lightweight, and bake evenly. They are equipped with a temperature gauge and a set of baking pans. I use these ovens in my cabin and in my base camps.

Here are some recipes you will want to try on your stove.

QUICK STEW

2 lbs. hamburger or equivalent in canned meatballs
4 cans condensed vegetable soup
½ stick margarine or ¼ cup oil

Ball the hamburger and brown it in oil or heat the meatballs. Pour undiluted soup over the meatballs and allow the mixture to heat thoroughly. Correct seasoning with salt and pepper. Serves 4 to 6.

CHIPPED BEEF ON BISCUITS

2 8-oz. packages chipped beef
2 cans cream soup—celery, mushroom, asparagus, cheese, or mix
⅜ cup milk

Combine undiluted soup, milk, and beef (you can use diced corned beef instead), and heat the mixture. Check flavor and add salt if needed. Serve over hot biscuits or bannock. Serves 2.

HURRY HASH

2 cans condensed cream of mushroom, celery, or other cream soup
4 sliced, hard-boiled eggs
biscuits, rusks, or melba toast
½ cup milk
2 cups diced canned ham loaf, corned beef, frankfurters,
 hamburgers, or the like

Heat soup slowly, stirring; add milk gradually. When smooth and hot, add meat and eggs. Heat and season if needed. Serve over biscuits. Serves 2 to 3.

Tip-Top Tuna

2 cans condensed cream of
  celery soup
1 7½-oz. can shredded tuna

2 tablespoons margarine
1 lb. noodles (or macaroni)
1 can peas

Boil noodles or macaroni as directed. Drain and add ¼ stick (2 tablespoons) margarine to coat noodles. Heat undiluted soup and add heated drained peas. Drain tuna; spread over noodles. Pour soup mixture over tuna, and heat over low heat until warm enough to serve. Serves 6 to 8.

Corn Chowder

8 slices bacon, cut into
  1-inch lengths
3 cups milk
4 medium potatoes

1 medium onion, minced
2 small cans whole kernel
  corn
1 teaspoon salt

Pare and dice potatoes into ¾-inch cubes. Boil with a tablespoon of onion in salted water. Meanwhile, fry bacon until light brown; remove and save. Fry balance of onion in fat until light yellow. Pour off all but a cup of the potato water when potatoes are cooked. Add bacon, onion, corn, and milk to potato pot and heat for 10 minutes. Do not boil. Serve over bannock or biscuits broken into each bowl. Serves 6.

Beef and Beans

1 lb. ground beef (lean)
1 package (6-oz.) noodles
2 cups water

1 package onion soup mix
1 can (1 lb. 11 oz.) green
  beans

Using stewing pot, sauté meat over low heat until browned. Drain off excess fat. Stir in onion soup mix, noodles, and 2 cups water (preferably hot). Cover and simmer over very low heat until noodles are almost tender. Drain beans; stir into mixture and continue simmering for about 5 minutes or until hot and noodles are tender. (Use bean liquor for extra liquid if necessary.) Serves 6 to 8.

BADLANDS GOULASH

6 medium potatoes, peeled and   2 onions, sliced
   diced   1 can (1 lb. 12 oz.) tomatoes
1 lb. polish sausages   salt and pepper
2 tablespoons bacon fat or oil

In stewing pot, simmer potatoes until tender, using as little water as possible. Slice sausages into bite-sized pieces; fry in bacon fat with onions until latter are light brown. Add tomatoes (including juice) and simmer. When potatoes are tender, drain if necessary, then stir into meat and tomato mixture. Season with salt and pepper to taste. Makes 6 servings.

PANHANDLE CHILI

1 can (1 lb. 12 oz.) tomatoes   1 can (12-oz.) corned beef
1 chopped onion or   chili pepper
   2 tablespoons dehydrated   1 can (1 lb. 14 oz.) kidney
   onion   beans

Mix tomatoes, corned beef, and onion; simmer over very low heat for 15 minutes. Stir in undrained beans. Add chili pepper to taste and simmer until heated through. Serves 6.

CAMPFIRE TUNA

1 package dehydrated spaghetti   ½ cup grated American cheese
   sauce mix   ½ cup water
1 can (1 lb. 12 oz.) tomatoes   1 teaspoon seasoned salt
1 package (8-oz.) egg noodles   1 can (13-oz.) tuna

Using small stewing pot, combine spaghetti sauce mix, tomatoes, water, and seasoned salt; blend thoroughly. Bring to a boil, reduce heat, cover, and simmer over very low heat for 20 minutes. Meanwhile cook noodles according to package directions until just tender. Drain. Stir in spaghetti sauce mixture, tuna, and cheese. Makes 6 to 8 servings.

HAM AND RED-EYE GRAVY

2 tablespoons butter or *water*
  margarine *¼ cup strong coffee*
1 slice ham about ¼-inch thick

Melt butter or margarine in skillet and fry ham until done. Remove to a platter and keep warm. Add a little water to the fat and coffee. Bring to a boil. Serve gravy over ham with grits. Serves 1 to 2.

CORN AND FRANK CHOWDER

2 tablespoons butter *3 frankfurters, thinly sliced*
1 can (1 lb.) whole kernel corn *2 cups milk*
2 cups water *1 teaspoon salt*
1 tablespoon instant minced *¼ teaspoon black pepper*
  onion
mashed potato granules ¼ cup
  (½ of 5-serving envelope)

Melt butter in large saucepan; add frankfurters and brown slightly. Stir in remaining ingredients; heat to boiling, stirring frequently. Reduce heat and simmer 5 minutes, stirring occasionally. If chowder is too thick, add some more milk or water. Makes 5 to 6 servings.

JOHNNY CAKE

2 eggs *2 teaspoons baking powder*
½ cup shortening *1 cup yellow corn meal*
1 cup sugar *2 cups all-purpose flour*
1½ teaspoons salt *1 teaspoon soda*
1 cup sour milk (add two tablespoons
  white vinegar to sweet milk to make
  sour milk or substitute buttermilk.)

Preheat oven to 350°F. In a large mixing bowl beat eggs. Blend in sugar and shortening. Add soda to sour milk and pour into the mixing bowl. Mix in corn meal. Slowly sift flour, baking powder, and salt into mixing bowl, stirring while doing so. When all ingredients are blended, pour into a greased iron skillet and bake in preheated oven for 45 minutes. Serves 2 to 3.

HIKER'S BEANS

2 cans (16 oz. each) baked beans
1 can (12 oz.) luncheon meat, cut into strips
2 tablespoons hot dog relish

In saucepan, combine ingredients and heat. Stir occasionally. Makes about 4½ cups.

RANGER'S RICE WITH BEEF

1 lb. ground beef
½ cup chopped onion
1 can (10 ¾ oz.) tomato soup
1½ cups quick-cooking rice, uncooked
½ teaspoon salt

½ cup chopped green pepper
1 large clove garlic, minced
1½ cups water
1 tablespoon Worcestershire sauce
generous dash pepper

In skillet, cook beef, green pepper, and onion with garlic until vegetables are tender (use shortening if necessary). Stir to separate meat. Add remaining ingredients. Bring to boil; reduce heat. Cover and cook 10 minutes or until liquid is absorbed. Stir occasionally. Makes about 5 cups.

PIONEER SOUP

1 can (11½ oz.) green pea soup
1 can (10¾ oz.) cream of potato soup
dash ground nutmeg

⅛ teaspoon thyme leaves, crushed
2 soup cans water or milk

In saucepan, blend soups; add milk (or water), thyme, and nutmeg. Heat; stir occasionally. Makes about 5 cups.

TRAIL SPAGHETTI

1 lb. ground beef
2 cups chopped onion
2 teaspoons basil leaves,
* crushed*
2 teaspoons oregano leaves,
* crushed*
4 cans (10¾ oz. each) tomato
* soup*

2 large cloves garlic, minced
2 cans (16 oz. each) tomatoes,
* cut up*
1 lb. spaghetti, cooked and
* drained*
grated Parmesan cheese

In saucepan, brown beef and cook onion with seasonings until onion is tender (use shortening if necessary). Stir to separate meat. Add soup and tomatoes. Simmer 1 hour and 15 minutes, stirring occasionally. Serve over spaghetti noodles with Parmesan. Makes about 7½ cups.

MOUNTAIN CHOWDER

½ cup sliced celery
½ cup chopped onion
2 tablespoons butter or
* margarine*
2 cans (10½ oz. each)
* chicken 'n dumplings soup*

1½ soup cans water
1 can (8 oz.) whole kernel
* corn, drained*
generous dash pepper

In saucepan, cook celery and onion in butter until tender. Add remaining ingredients. Heat; stir occasionally. Makes about 5½ cups.

FRYPAN BURGWICHES

1 lb. ground beef
½ cup chopped onion
1 can (10¾ oz.) chicken gumbo,
* tomato, or vegetable soup*
hamburger buns, split and
* toasted*

1 tablespoon prepared
* mustard*
dash pepper

In skillet, brown beef and cook onion (use shortening if necessary). Stir to separate meat; pour off fat. Add soup and seasonings. Heat; stir occasionally. Serve on buns. Makes about 3 cups.

COMPASS FRANKS

8 frankfurters, split lengthwise
2 tablespoons butter or
* margarine*
2 cans (11¼ oz. each)
* chili beef soup*

⅔ cup water
8 frankfurter rolls, split and
* toasted*

In skillet, brown frankfurters in butter. Add soup and water. Heat; stir occasionally. Place frankfurters in rolls; spoon chili over. Garnish with chopped onion if desired. Makes 8 sandwiches.

HIGH SIERRA SKILLET

1 lb. ground beef
½ cup chopped onion
¼ cup chopped green pepper
1 can (10¾ oz.) tomato soup
1½ cups whole kernel corn

½ teaspoon salt
¼ teaspoon oregano leaves,
* crushed*
generous dash pepper

In skillet, brown beef and cook onion and green pepper until tender (use shortening if necessary). Stir to separate meat; pour off fat. Add remaining ingredients. Cook over low heat a few minutes to blend flavors. Stir occasionally. Makes about 4 cups.

ROUNDUP SCRAMBLED EGGS

1 can (10 ¾ oz.) cream of celery,
* chicken, or mushroom soup*
2 tablespoons butter or
* margarine*

8 eggs, slightly beaten
dash pepper

In bowl, stir soup until smooth; gradually blend in eggs and pepper. In 10-inch skillet, melt butter; pour in egg mixture. Cook over low heat without stirring. As mixture begins to set around edges, gently lift cooked portions with large spatula so that thin, un-cooked portions can flow to the bottom. Continue gently lifting cooked portions until eggs are completely set, but still moist—about 8 minutes. Makes 4 servings.

COWPOKE SPAGHETTI

1 can (12 oz.) luncheon meat,   *¼ cup chopped onion*
cubed   *2 tablespoons chopped parsley*
2 tablespoons butter or   *(optional)*
margarine
1 can (26½ oz.) spaghetti in tomato sauce with cheese

In saucepan, brown luncheon meat and cook onion in butter until tender. Add spaghetti and parsley. Heat; stir occasionally. Makes about 4 cups.

CAMPSITE GRAVY

Add 1 can (10¾ oz.) cream of celery, chicken, mushroom, or golden mushroom soup to 2 to 4 tablespoons meat drippings (or butter) in pan. Blend in ¼ to ⅓ cup water. Heat; stir often. Makes about 1½ cups.

GOOD NIGHT SPECIAL

Try this creamy drink as a perfect way to end the day. It is even better with a little bourbon or brandy. Mix:

1 packet hot chocolate mix   *3 heaping teaspoons powdered*
1 heaping teaspoon instant   *milk*
coffee   *1 cup boiling water*

I have a very good Cajun friend down in the swamps of Louisiana who guides me on bowfishing trips for gar. Fritz Dietlien is one of the most interesting people with whom I have had the opportunity to explore the backcountry. Fritz has been credited with giving the meaning of the word adventure as "misery at a distance." He is one of the best wood stove chefs found. Here are two of his garfish recipes you may want to try on your sheepherder's stove.

GARFISH PATTIES OR BALLS (*BOULETTES*)

1 10-lb. gar (or any saltwater   *chopped garlic*
fish)   *parsley*
salt to taste   *bread crumbs*

pepper to taste
red potatoes (⅓ potato to ⅔ fish)
flour
3 eggs
chopped onion and onion tops
(Note: seasonings should be about ½ of potato amount.)

Parboil cleaned fish so fish will flake with a fork; add salt and pepper to taste. Boil potatoes. Chop seasonings.

Mix fish, seasonings, and potatoes that have been mashed with the eggs.

Make into patties or balls (makes about 10 balls/patties), turn in plain flour, and pan or deep fry in oil. Serves 6.

GARFISH COURT BOUILLON

5 lbs. fish (any kind)
salt to taste
pepper to taste
3 cups diced onion
1 cup bell pepper, diced
6 cloves diced garlic
1 cup diced celery
onion tops
1 can tomato paste
1 teaspoon sugar
3 cans stewed tomatoes (can use Ro-Tel)
4 or 5 lemon slices
water or beer

Fillet fish and cut into cubes. Season with salt and pepper to taste and put into refrigerator.

Dice onion, bell pepper, garlic, and onion tops (save some tops to add 5 minutes before serving).

Add tomato paste and sugar to seasonings in heavy iron or aluminum pot and stir over medium fire until paste browns. When it has turned a rusty brown color, add stewed tomatoes or Ro-Tel. Mash tomatoes and allow to cook about 2 hours, adding water or beer to keep liquid level up.

Add fish and allow to cook 20 to 30 minutes. Five minutes before serving, add 4 or 5 slices of lemon and a handful of onion tops. You may need additional salt or pepper to taste. Eat with rice or garlic bread. Five lbs. of fish cooked this way will serve 8.

Bannock—Bread of the Wilderness

U p in the North Country the seventeenth-century French-Canadian voyagers opened up the wilderness from the Great Lakes to north central Canada with their trapping operations. These great canoeists traveled vast distances on light rations. One of their main staples was bannock, a simple bread of Scottish descent. Bannock has been the bread of the wilderness traveler for centuries in the cold North Country and is still very popular among those who spend most of their time in the backcountry.

Several winters ago I spent some time with a Canadian backcountry trapper studying his trail cooking techniques. The old-timer was dedicated to the simple life and did all of his cooking on an open fire. I learned from this delightful old trapper many varied ways of using bannock. Much of this chapter was taken from his teachings.

The following recipes will show you how to make a basic bannock mix and several of the ways this basic mix can be used on the trail or at home. The basic mix is given here in one-person proportions. It can be mixed in advance and will stay fresh for six weeks or more if kept covered, sealed, dry, and cool. Sealable plastic bags are good for storing and carrying on the trail.

BASIC BANNOCK

1 cup all-purpose flour
¼ teaspoon salt
2 tablespoons powdered skim milk

1 teaspoon double-action
baking powder

A Bannock mix is easy to carry on the trail.

BANNOCK BREAD

Cooking the bread in camp or in your fireplace is simple. Grease your skillet and let it get warm by the fire. Add enough cold water to the bannock mix to make a soft dough. Mold this rapidly, with as little handling as possible, into a cake about 1 inch thick and lay it into the hot pan.

The reason for handling the bannock as little as possible is that when liquid is added to the dry bannock mix, it releases gas from the baking powder. This gas causes the dough to rise. Rough handling can cause the gas to escape, leaving you with flat, hard bread. It is in-

A cast iron skillet propped on a rock is what is needed to bake bannock. *Photo by J. Wayne Fears.*

teresting to note that cold water releases the gas much more slowly than warm, giving more time to form the bread and get it into the pan.

Once the bannock is in the pan, hold it over the fire until a crust forms on the bottom, then turn it over. At this stage prop the skillet at a steep angle in front of the fire so that the loaf will receive a lot of heat on top. When it looks golden brown, test by sticking a twig in the loaf. If the dough sticks, the loaf needs to cook longer. After you have cooked bannock awhile, you will learn to tap it with your finger and gauge by the hollow sound when it is done. Cooking time is usually about 15 minutes.

If your canoe turns over and you lose your skillet but manage to save the bannock mix, you can prepare it on a stick. Mix the bannock into a stiff dough, using less water than usual. Press the dough flat and cut into 1-inch strips. Wind these spirally around a green hickory or a sassafras stick. Hold over a bed of coals, turning the stick so that the bread browns evenly.

Bannock can also be cooked in a Dutch oven, reflector oven, sheepherder's stove, or on your stove at home.

BANNOCK PANCAKES

2 cups of basic bannock mix
1 tablespoon freeze-dried
  scrambled egg mixture

1 large handful of raisins
water

Mix ingredients with water. Two cups of water will usually be right. Do not beat until smooth since lumps disappear during baking and beating toughens pancakes. Grease frying pan lightly, pour in batter, and cook slowly, turning only once. Serve with honey. Usually serves 4.

BEEF STEW WITH BANNOCK DUMPLINGS

1 package freeze-dried beef stew
1 package onion soup mix
water

1 package freeze-dried peas
1 cup bannock mix

Empty beef stew and other ingredients into large pot; add 5 to 6 cups of water (more if you like your stew thinner). Bring to boil. Mix 1 cup bannock mix with ⅓ cup water; drop into boiling stew. Cover tightly with lid or foil. Cook for 15 minutes without uncovering. Be careful that fire is not too hot under the pot because it can burn the stew. Usually serves 4.

BANNOCK HAMBURGER PIE

2 packages freeze-dried hamburgers, finely crumbled
3 to 4 tablespoons dried onion flakes
salt, pepper, catsup to taste
2 cups bannock mix
water

Soak hamburgers in warm water with spices as directed. Do not brown. Add the onion flakes, and let soak for the required time.

Mix bannock as directed in the bannock bread recipe and divide into 2 balls. Lightly grease frying pan and pat one of the bannock balls over the surface. Add meat mixture, salt, pepper, and catsup if desired.

Cover with second bannock ball; flatten and push down at the sides to seal. Bake carefully, turning with saucer and pancake spatula to give support. Usually serves 4.

BANNOCK FISH STICKS

4 to 6 fish fillets   *1 tablespoon dried onion flakes*
2 cups bannock mix   *Salt, pepper, small amount*
water   *butter*

Cook fish fillets and onion in small amount of salted boiling water for about 2 minutes. Remove fish and as much of the onion as possible with a slotted spoon. Flake fish with fork, add salt, pepper, and a small amount of butter.

Mix bannock and pat out as thinly as possible. Cut or tear into individual squares, put fish mixture into middle, and seal edges by pinching together. Fry in butter, or bake as for bread. Serves 4 to 6.

BANNOCK STRAWBERRY SHORTCAKE

Shortcakes
Mix 2 cups bannock mix with water until a soft dough ball forms. Cook bannock on one side. After turning, sprinkle liberally with white sugar.

Topping

1 package freeze-dried strawberries
1 package Dream Whip
water
1 tablespoon powdered milk

Soak the strawberries in water or orange juice using a little less water than called for.

Mix Dream Whip with 1 large tablespoon of powdered milk and ½ cup of water. Beat with fork for about 2 minutes or until thick. Cut sugared bannock into 4 squares, pour or spoon on fruit, and spoon Dream Whip over all. Serves 4.

BANNOCK CINNAMON ROLLS

2 cups of basic bannock mix   *brown sugar and cinnamon*
water   *1 large handful of raisins*

Bake bannock as directed in bread recipe. After turning once, sprinkle cooked side with raisins, brown sugar, and cinnamon.

Serve with cooked apricots and hot coffee. Serves 3 to 4.

BANNOCK CABIN CAKE

1 package Dream Whip   *2 cups bannock mix*
1 cup water   *1 large handful granola*

Prepare dough by combining bannock mix and water. Cook bannock in frying pan over lower heat than when making regular bannock. After turning once, sprinkle cooked side with granola; spoon on Dream Whip. Serves 2.

Variations

After turning once, sprinkle cooked side with honey and granola, or peanut butter and granola, or additional dried fruit, granola, and Dream Whip.

This simple cake tastes good after a day on snowshoes or cross-country skis.

APRICOT SHORTCAKE

1 cup dried apricots   *1 teaspoon Tang (opt.)*
slivered almonds or walnuts   *3 to 4 teaspoons sugar (opt.)*
1 package Dream Whip   *1 tablespoon powdered milk*
1 bannock shortcake   *water*

Chop dried apricots and cover with water. Add teaspoon of Tang and 3 or 4 teaspoons of sugar, depending on how tart you like your apricots. Simmer until tender. Add nuts.

Pour fruit over bannock shortcake. Mix Dream Whip with powdered milk and ½ cup of water. Beat with fork for about 2 minutes or until thick. Spoon topping onto shortcake. Serves 3 to 4.

Sourdough—Bread of Legend

History books dealing with the adventurous era of gold strikes in Alaska and the Yukon are full of references to sourdough bread and pancakes. In fact, another word for an Alaskan old-timer is "sourdough". However, my introduction to sourdough was not on the frontier of Alaska, but at a remote ranch high in the Ruby Mountains of northeastern Nevada. It was my first mule-deer hunt and I was packing into the Big Thorpe area with Lloyd Blume. Lloyd, who looked like he stepped out of a Zane Grey novel, had spent a long lifetime roaming the wilderness areas of Montana, Idaho, and Nevada. He still lived the remote life of a western rancher and hunting guide, with few modern conveniences. However, his wife's cooking didn't need any help from modern specialized appliances. It was delicious by any standards.

The first morning of the hunt no one had to wake me; the sweet bread-like aroma drifting into my room got my attention, even in my deep sleep. I got up, dressed, and sneaked into the kitchen to find the source of this delightful alarm clock.

"Sit down, Wayne," Mrs. Blume said with a smile, "and have a stack of sourdough pancakes." I had read of sourdough, but this was my first real sample. Three stacks later I wondered if I could still get on my horse. They had tasted just as delectable as they smelled.

The last time I saw the Blumes, they were still laughing about that country boy from back East who spent a week trying to eat up their supply of sourdough. Since that introduction to sourdough cooking many years ago, I have been a true fan of anything made from it.

Several modern-day breads have been somehow dubbed sourdough, but Don Holm, an outdoor writer and wilderness cooking expert from Oregon, states that true sourdough is simply homemade yeast—a form of fermented dough used as a leavening in bread making, which has been a part of the art of cooking for several thousand years.

In many remote backcountry cabins today, a sourdough starter is the most important possession in a homesteader's outfit—something to cherish and guard. The starter is the basis of almost every meal. As Don states, "From it one can manufacture not only bread, biscuits, and flapjacks, but feed the dogs, apply to burns and wounds, chink the log cabin, brew hootch and, some say, even resole boots." I have also found that you can tan small animal skins with it.

Much of the information in this chapter I have obtained from my trips to Alaska and from the Cooperative Extension Service of the University of Alaska. Their home economists have refined sourdough cooking into a science. Here is their version of how sourdough became an Alaskan legend.

In the early days of Alaska, bread making at home was a necessity. Food supplies came only once or twice a year by ship and then were transferred to small boats, river steamers, dog sleds, or backpacks to reach their destination. Many localities received supplies only when a steamer could navigate the river or the lake during the few months of summer thaw. Orders placed the year before required careful selection and close attention to quantities, since the timing en route proved uncertain.

Yeast supplies ran out and replacements could be a long time in coming, especially if unusual ice formations and heavy winds or seas delayed the ship's entry into rivers or ports of call. So the sourdough-starter method evolved, keeping a continuous supply of leavened dough handy. Ordinary yeast plants, sensitive to the extreme cold, refused to grow well, while the combination of wild or adapted yeast in the sourdough starter proved tough.

SOURDOUGH STARTER

For best results, use glass or pottery containers. Never use a metal container or leave a metal spoon in the starter. A good starter contains only flour, water, and yeast. It has a clean sour odor. The liquid will separate from the batter when it stands several days, but this does not matter.

Commercial sourdough starters are dried and powdered. Adding water brings them to life. In growing, the yeast gives off carbon dioxide that forms bubbles in sourdough or any other yeast dough. Soda is added to react with the acids resulting from the action of the yeast, thus forming more gas and making the batter lighter. If too much soda is added, the product is brownish when baked. If too little soda is used, the product may be too sour in taste. Add the soda just before baking. In any sourdough recipe, it is helpful to reserve one tablespoon of the liquid to dissolve the soda. Add this to the batter last, mix thoroughly, and bake. Never add soda to the starter, since it kills the yeast.

To start a sourdough pot, you may be fortunate enough to share one of the starters handed down over the years. Or you may wish to make your own starter.

HOMEMADE SOURDOUGH STARTER

In a bowl mix well:

2 cups flour   *2 cups warm water*
1 package dry yeast or 1 yeast cake

Place in a warm location or closed cupboard overnight. In the morning put ½ cup of the starter in a scalded pint jar, cover, and store in the refrigerator or a cool place for future use. Leave lots of room for expansion in the container, or set the lid on without tightening it. This is sourdough starter. The remaining batter can be used immediately for pancakes, waffles, muffins, bread, or cake.

Starter will keep almost indefinitely in a clean, covered glass container in the refrigerator. If unused for several weeks, the starter may need to sit out an extra night before flour and water are added to stand overnight for use.

Sourdough starter may be dried for easy storing or sharing. To dry, drop by teaspoonfuls onto wax paper. Turn frequently until completely dry. Drying takes about 24 hours. Store in a covered jar. To reconstitute, crumble 2 or 3 circles of starter in ½ cup of warm water. Let stand overnight or until bubbly. Add ½ cup water and ½ cup flour. Stir. Let stand overnight or until bubbly. Use as directed in recipes.

The original sourdough users would add enough flour to their starter to shape it into a ball and then put it in a sack of flour for easy carrying. Some Alaskans are still using a starter traced back to an original pot brought into the country with the gold rush. To them the sourdough pot is a prized possession. I am also told that there is a starter being used in a San Francisco restaurant that dates back to 1850, when it was first mixed.

To increase your supply of starter for sharing, set the sponge out as if you were planning to make sourdough hotcakes the following day. In the morning, instead of adding eggs, sugar, and other ingredients, remove your portion of starter as usual, then either dry as directed above, or place other portions of the starter in clean glass or pottery containers for sharing.

SOURDOUGH PANCAKES

Sourdough pancakes, the main breakfast dish of prospectors, miners, and old-time Alaskans, differ from other pancakes in that the batter is leavened with a yeast starter and soda. The starter must be set out the night before it is to be used.

The recipes below can easily be made with a Dutch oven or reflector oven in your fireplace, as well as a conventional gas or electric oven.

Measurements are not precise. If you prefer a thin pancake, add another egg or a bit more water. Of course, for a thicker cake the batter should be thicker. At the time of baking, the batter for sourdough should be the same consistency as the batter for other pancakes that are family favorites.

Set aside a ½ cup sponge of sourdough starter in the refrigerator jar for next time. To remaining sponge add:

1 or 2 eggs
1 tablespoon oil
1 teaspoon soda dissolved in 1 tablespoon water
1 teaspoon salt
1 tablespoon sugar

Beat with a fork and blend in all ingredients. If you like, add several tablespoons of nonfat dry milk powder to any of the sourdough recipes at this point for extra nutrition. Add soda/water mixture just before baking. Bake on a hot griddle. Turn once. Serve with a mixture of hot brown-sugar syrup or honey and melted butter. Molasses, jelly, or rose hip syrup are other tasty toppings. For interesting variations add ½ cup whole-wheat flour, cornmeal, wheat germ, or bran flakes to the batter. (Two eggs will provide the liquid for this addition.) Serves 3.

SOURDOUGH WAFFLES

Use the basic pancake recipe, but add 2 extra tablespoons of oil. Add the fat, then the soda/water mixture and bake at once, according to the directions that come with your waffle iron.

SOURDOUGH MUFFINS

In the evening, or 6 to 8 hours before using, set out the sponge as for pancakes. In the morning save ½ cup for next starter, as usual, and to the remaining sponge add:

1 teaspoon salt
¼ cup nonfat dry milk
½ cup melted fat or oil
1 or 2 eggs
1 teaspoon soda dissolved in 1
  tablespoon water

1 to 1½ cups whole wheat
  flour
¾ cup raisins (optional)
½ cup sugar

Sift dry ingredients into a bowl. Make a well in the center. Mix egg and fat thoroughly with the sponge. Add this to the well in the flour. Stir only enough to moisten the flour. Add the soda/water mixture just before filling muffin tins. Addition ¾ cup raisins, blueberries, or cranberries for a special treat. Fill greased muffin tins ¾ full. Bake in 375°F oven for 30 to 35 minutes. Yields 20 small or 12 large muffins.

SOURDOUGH BREAD

Set out sponge as for pancakes and let stand in a warm place overnight or for 6 to 8 hours. Save ½ cup for next starter. To the remaining sponge, which should be about 2 cups, add:

4 cups sifted flour (or more)
2 tablespoons fat or oil
(¼ teaspoon soda and 1 tablespoon water added later)

2 tablespoons sugar
1 teaspoon salt

Sift dry ingredients into a bowl, making a well in the center. Add fat to the sponge and mix well. Pour into the well of flour. Add enough flour to make a soft dough for kneading. Knead on a floured board for 10 to 15 minutes. Place in a greased bowl. Cover with a towel and let rise in a warm place for 2 to 4 hours or until doubled. Dissolve the ¼ teaspoon of soda in a tablespoon of warm water and add to the dough. Knead it in thoroughly. Shape dough into 2 loaves in bread pans and set aside to rise. When doubled, bake at 375°F for 50 to 60 minutes.

SOURDOUGH FRENCH BREAD

Prepare as above (but with a package—1 tablespoon—of yeast added to the starter). Shape into 2 loaves by dividing the dough in half. Roll each half into a 15″ × 12″ rectangle. Wind up tightly toward you, beginning with the wide side. Seal edges by pinching together. Place rolls diagonally on greased baking sheets that have been lightly sprinkled with cornmeal. Let rise until doubled, about 1 hour. Brush with cold water. Cut with scissors or knife to make 1 or 2 lengthwise or several diagonal ¼-inch deep slits across tops of loaves. Place in a hot (400°F) oven with a pan of boiling water. Bake 15 minutes. Remove from oven and brush again with water. Reduce the temperature to 350°F and bake 35 to 40 minutes until golden brown. Brush a third time with cold water and bake 2 to 3 minutes longer. Makes 2 French loaves.

SOURDOUGH WHEAT

2 cups sourdough starter (set out the previous night)
1 cup whole wheat or graham flour
1 cup white flour
2 tablespoons sugar
1½ teaspoons salt

Combine ingredients and mix well with a fork—this sponge will be sticky. Set in a warm cupboard for 2 hours or more. Turn out on a warm, well-floured board. Knead 1 or more cups white flour into the dough for 5 to 10 minutes. Shape into a round loaf and place in a well-greased pie pan. Grease sides and top of loaf, cover with a towel, and let rise 1 hour or until doubled. Bake in a preheated oven at 450°F for 10 minutes, then reduce heat to 375°F and bake 30 to 40 minutes longer. Makes 1 large loaf. (If starter is very sour, add ¼ teaspoon soda to the flour that is kneaded in on the board.

CASSEROLE BREAD

Use same ingredients and method as for sourdough bread. Do not knead the dough, but beat it 2 minutes at medium speed of electric mixer or 300 strokes by hand. Let stand in mixing bowl until double in bulk. Add ¼ teaspoon soda; mix ½ minute, turn into greased casserole or loaf pan, and let stand for 40 minutes. Bake as for sourdough bread. Bread is done when crust sounds hollow when tapped. Makes 1 large loaf.

Variations

Substitute 1 cup whole wheat for 1 cup of the white flour; use honey, brown sugar, or light molasses instead of sugar, or the juice of one orange and the grated orange rind for orange bread.

SOURDOUGH CHOCOLATE CAKE

½ cup thick starter	*1 cup water*
1½ cups flour	*¼ cup nonfat dry milk*

Mix and let ferment 2 to 3 hours in a warm place until bubbly and there is a clean sour milk odor. Add:

1 teaspoon cinnamon	*1 cup sugar*
1½ teaspoons soda	*½ cup shortening*
2 eggs	*½ teaspoon salt*
3 squares melted chocolate	*1 teaspoon vanilla*

Cream shortening, sugar, flavorings, salt, and soda. Add eggs one at a time, beating well after each addition. Combine creamed mixture and melted chocolate with sourdough mixture. Stir 300 strokes or mix at low speed until blended. Pour into 2 layer pans or 1 larger pan. Bake at 350°F for 25 to 30 minutes. Cool and frost with butterscotch-chocolate frosting or other icing of your choice.

BUTTERSCOTCH-CHOCOLATE FROSTING

3 1-oz. squares of unsweetened chocolate
¼ cup brown sugar, firmly packed
¼ teaspoon salt
vanilla (1 to 2 teaspoons) to taste
Confectioner's sugar (approximately 3 cups)

In a saucepan, combine unsweetened chocolate, brown sugar, and ¼ teaspoon salt. Bring to boil, stirring constantly; cook until chocolate is melted, then remove from heat. Add vanilla and enough confectioners' sugar for good spreading consistency (about 3 cups). Spread over sides and top of cake. Enough frosting for a 2-layer cake or a large sheet cake.

Make Your Own Jerky

Early explorers in North America found that they needed a lightweight, nutritional trail food that required no special storage. From the Indians they learned how to make one that met these requirements. It was called jerky. Today those who enjoy backcountry activities have somewhat the same requirements as those of the earlier explorers—to travel light, but to eat well. We can still depend on homemade jerky.

Jerky is easy to make and carries well in the field.

I have been on extended expeditions over much of the world where jerky was a basic food while traveling, and it performs as well as a trail food today as it did two hundred years ago. I enjoy it in my lunch at home and on the trail while canoeing or backpacking.

Jerky can easily be made in your home kitchen using your oven. It makes a good rainy Saturday project. Almost any lean cut of beef, venison, elk, caribou, or moose can be made into jerky; however, the cheaper cuts of beef such as round steak work just as well. Jerky is high in protein and supplies energy without adding pounds to your weight. Besides being an excellent trail food, jerky is good in stews. Simply mix the jerky into the pot with the rest of the stew ingredients. The jerky will quickly absorb moisture during cooking and will enlarge to become plump, tender pieces of meat.

Here are several ways you can make jerky.

BASIC JERKY

Cut the meat into 6-inch strips about ½ inch wide and ¼ inch thick. Be sure to cut the strips with the grain running lengthwise; this keeps the jerky from breaking easily. Trim off all the fat since it will turn rancid. Then season the strips with salt and pepper. Brush on Liquid Smoke.

Stick a round toothpick through one end of each strip.

Place a layer of aluminum foil in the oven to catch the drippings. Suspend the strips from the top oven rack. Turn the heat on to 160°F. Leave the oven door slightly open so the moisture can escape. Heat for approximately 6 to 8 hours or until the meat turns dark and there is no moisture in the center of the strip.

When the strips are done they should be completely dry but flexible enough to bend without breaking. Remove them from the oven, take the toothpicks out, and store the strips in a re-sealable plastic bag.

CABIN JERKY

2 lbs. meat
½ cup water
¼ teaspoon garlic powder

1 envelope teriyaki sauce mix
¼ teaspoon salt
¼ teaspoon lemon-pepper
    seasoning

Stick a toothpick through each piece of jerky and suspend from oven rack.

Cut off all fat from meat. Slice with grain into slices about ¼ inch thick. Check that all fat is removed. Pour contents of sauce envelope into small bowl, add water, and stir well. Add salt, garlic powder, and lemon-pepper seasoning and stir. Place strips of meat into mixing bowl and toss with sauce to thoroughly cover meat.

Place wire rack on top of cookie sheet and place meat on rack. Meat slices may touch but should not overlap. Place rack in very slow oven (160°F) and cook for 10 to 12 hours with door ajar. Remove meat and place in airtight container.

QUICK JERKY

Remove all fat from meat. Cut to any size strips, not over ¼ to ½ inch thick.

Rub into each strip Morton's (Smoke Flavored) Sugar Cure. Place in oven on rack and set oven between 160°F and 200°F. Leave door ajar so moisture can escape, and dry meat to taste. After strips are dried, you may paint them on each side with Liquid Smoke or A1 Sauce for added flavor.

SALTED JERKY

Prepare brine of 2½ cups pickling salt and 3 quarts of water. Add meat strips and soak for 1 to 2 days. Remove meat and wipe dry.

Drape salted strips or suspend by string or wire loops on wood frame about 5 feet above small, slow, smoky fire of any non-resinous wood. (Be careful that fire is not too hot or it will cook meat. Fire adds smoky taste to jerky and discourages insects.) Cover meat at night and during rain. Depending upon weather, jerky should be done in 24 to 48 hours.

SEASONED JERKY

1 flank steak (approximately
  1½ lbs.)
⅛ teaspoon garlic powder
1 teaspoon monosodium
  glutamate

¼ cup soy sauce
1 teaspoon seasoned salt
⅛ teaspoon black pepper
1 teaspoon onion powder
¼ cup Worcestershire sauce

Trim all fat from meat and partially freeze. Cut with grain into ⅛ to ¼ inch thick slices. Combine seasonings. Combine sauces. Stir sauce into seasonings, then combine all. Cover bottom of 9″×15″×2″ Pyrex dish with sauce. Place one layer of flank strips in sauce. Brush on more sauce. Cover with more strips of meat. Brush on remaining sauce. Marinate overnight. Lay strips of marinated meat in single layer on oven racks (place foil underneath to catch drips). Dry at 160°F for 6 to 8 hours, until chewy as desired. Taste occasionally. Makes approximately ½ lb.

Recipe can be doubled or tripled if there is room in the oven. (Pieces must not overlap.) Seasonings given will be enough for one flank steak. If you wish, try 1 teaspoon Liquid Smoke or cooking sherry. Remember to leave door ajar while drying to allow moisture to escape.

VENISON JERKY

Cut 1½ to 2 lbs. venison into strips (with grain) 6 inches long, 1½ inches wide, and ½ inch thick. Set aside. Mix together the following:

1 package instant meat marinade
½ teaspoon Liquid Smoke

¾ cup cold water
¼ teaspoon garlic powder

¼ teaspoon onion powder   *¼ teaspoon black pepper*
½ teaspoon red pepper sauce

Place meat in container and cover with marinade, piercing slices deeply with fork. Marinate overnight in covered container in refrigerator. Remove meat strips, drain slightly, and place onto rack, making sure strips do not overlap. Place rack over cookie sheet in a 150°F to 175°F oven and bake for 8 to 10 hours leaving door slightly ajar to allow moisture to escape. Remove from oven, cool, and store in an airtight container.

BEEF JERKY

1½ lbs. flank steak, partially   *¼ cup Worcestershire sauce*
   frozen   *1 teaspoon salt*
1 teaspoon Liquid Smoke   *⅓ teaspoon garlic powder*
⅓ teaspoon ground black   *½ teaspoon monosodium*
   pepper   *glutamate*
1 teaspoon onion powder   *¼ cup soy sauce*

Slice flank steak into thick slices diagonally across the grain.

Combine seasonings and brush onto both sides of meat. Arrange meat slices on two 10″ × 15″ × 1″ jelly-roll pans.

Place in preheated, very low (200°F) oven for 8 to 12 hours with door ajar to allow moisture to escape. Turn meat several times to dry out evenly, or hang outside on string, away from animals, in cool, airy place to dry.

Store in plastic bags. Makes ¾ lb.

ALASKAN JERKY

3 lbs. venison, reindeer, caribou   *½ teaspoon Liquid Smoke*
   or moose   *salt and pepper to taste*
2 tablespoons water

Slice meat ¼ inch thick and remove all fat. Lay out in single layer on a counter surface. Dab each piece with a brush dipped in water and Liquid Smoke. Salt generously. Do not use iodized salt. Sprinkle with pepper if desired.

Place strips, layer on layer, into a large bowl or crock. Put a plate and weight on top. Let stand overnight or at least 6 hours. Remove meat strips from bowl and dry.

Remove oven racks. Stretch meat strips across racks. Allow edges to touch but not overlap. Do not cover entire rack. Leave door slightly ajar to allow moisture to escape. Arrange racks so that top rack is not closer than 4 inches from the top source of heat and bottom rack no closer than 4 inches from bottom of oven.

Set oven temperature for 160°F and let the meat dry for about 11 hours. Check early in the drying process. If there is excessive drip, catch it on aluminum foil on a rack near the bottom of the oven.

Cool the jerky and store in an airtight container. Makes 1 lb.

HOMESTEADERS' JERKY

Round steak, with the fat trimmed off, is recommended for making this jerky. With a sharp knife cut the round steak into slices ¼ inch thick, ¾ inches wide and 10 inches long. Using the blunt edge of a cup, pound the strips as thin as possible being careful not to tear them apart. Using a wire basket strainer lower the strips into a pan of heavily salted, boiling water; leave the strips in the water about 15 seconds, just enough to blanch the meat. Take out and place on paper towels to drain. Salt to taste with hickory salt.

Construct a cylinder out of cheesecloth, about 3 feet long and 12 inches in diameter. You will also need a piece of nylon cord about 6 feet long. Using a large needle and strong white cotton thread, pierce the cord near one end, then pierce a piece of jerky near one end; then pierce the cord again about 1 inch away from the first point, and so on. In this manner, sew the jerky to the cord. Now slip the cheesecloth cylinder over the sewn jerky and shut a clothespin over each end of the cylinder to keep out the flies.

Carry the jerky outside, holding onto the 2 ends of the cord that protrude from the cheesecloth cylinder, and fasten the line of jerky between 2 tree limbs where animals cannot reach it. Select a place in the sunlight. If it rains, cover the jerky or take it inside. Leave it in the open for about 5 days and you will have finished jerky. It will get stiff and very dark.

SMOKED JERKY

Freeze a flank or top round steak until almost solid. Remove from freezer and cut into thin strips, trimming off all fat. Cut strips into 4- to 5-inch lengths and put in heavy duty plastic bag. Pour in enough bottled teriyaki sauce to just cover meat strips. Turn bag to coat all pieces of meat. Refrigerate several hours or overnight. Lift meat out of marinade and arrange on cooking grill in a smoker. Cover and smoke about 6 hours or until meat is completely dried and almost brittle. Cool, then store in tightly covered container.

SWEET JERKY

1 cup soy sauce
2 teaspoons honey
1 teaspoon finely diced garlic
2 lbs. round or flank steak

pepper
1 teaspoon ground ginger
1 teaspoon finely diced onion

Warm soy sauce slightly to help dissolve honey. Stir all ingredients together and marinate strips of meat several hours or overnight. Cut meat 1 inch thick with the grain. Put foil under the rack in the oven to catch drippings. Lay strips of meat onto the rack and liberally sprinkle with lemon-marinated (or fresh ground) pepper. Bake for 5 hours at 160°F. Makes ¾ lb.

SPORTSMAN'S JERKY

venison or lean beef
sugar
Liquid Smoke

seasoning salt
pepper

Trim all the fat from the meat. Cut the meat into strips 1 to 2 inches wide, ¼ inch thick, and 8 to 10 inches long. Place a layer of the strips in a glass cooking dish. Sprinkle a mixture of 3 parts sugar, 3 parts seasoning salt, and 2 parts black pepper. Sprinkle on some Liquid Smoke. Put another layer of meat on top of the first and sprinkle again with seasonings. Continue this process until all the meat has been treated.

Cover meat and let it stand in the refrigerator for 6 to 8 hours or overnight. After taking the meat out of the refrigerator, cover an oven rack with aluminum foil and evenly space the meat strips on the foil. Put into oven at 160°F and bake until the meat is completely dry, about 8 hours, but longer if required. Store in airtight container.

SALMON JERKY

Slice salmon fillets into thin strips. (Any saltwater fish may be used.) Salt fish in a dish or enameled pan using 2 tablespoons salt per pound. Refrigerate for 12 hours. Remove from the refrigerator and place strips onto a rack in the oven to dry. Set the oven to the lowest possible temperature and allow meat to dehydrate for 3 to 5 hours, leaving the door slightly ajar to allow moisture to escape.

The salmon strips may also be dried in the sun; the process takes about 3 days. The meat should be brought in at night to prevent moisture condensation.

CHAPTER

11

Trail Foods You Can Make Ahead

D id you ever wonder how the Indians, explorers, and pio-
neers of early North America survived the vast wilderness
areas? There were no country stores, cities, or trading posts
in which to purchase foods for trail use. These early wanderers cre-
ated trail foods that could be made up before the trip and carried
with them on their long journeys. Today we can travel the backcountry utilizing many of these time-tested trail foods as well as
some new creations. During my career in the outdoors, I have
searched out the best of the trail foods and have lived with them
under wilderness conditions.

Not only are these trail foods good while traveling in the backcountry, but they are also delicious surprises in a school lunch box
or for snacking on at home.

The best known trail food is jerky, to which I have devoted a
whole chapter of this book. However, it is interesting to note that
early American Indians found that they could not live on jerky
alone since it supplied only protein with few vitamins. In order to
balance their diet they melted animal fat and added crushed berries,
nuts, and shredded jerky. The mixture was poured into bags made
of animal membrane and the cooled results were called pemmican.

Our history is rich in accolades to pemmican. Alexander
MacKenzie cached pemmican in grass and bark-lined holes in the
ground for his return trip during the first crossing of North America.
America's greatest hunting trip, the Lewis and Clark Expedition, depended upon pemmican for trail food. Admiral Peary's journey to
the North Pole was accomplished with pemmican as the staple

food, which Peary and his men ate cold, twice a day. The admiral wrote that it was the "most satisfying food I know."

ORIGINAL PEMMICAN

jerky   *rendered lard*
powdered, dried, tart berries

Combine equal parts of jerky, berries, and lard. Roll pemmican into 1″ × 3″ rolls, or pat into muffin tins or paper cups and wrap in foil to carry on the trail.

MODERN PEMMICAN

1 cup dried peaches   *1 cup coconut*
1 cup dried apples   *½ cup dried prunes*
1 cup dried raisins   *1 cup chopped peanuts*

More dried fruit may be added or substitutions made for any of the above if desired. Put all the ingredients through a food grinder at least twice. Blend well. Bind the ingredients together by mixing in the following:

½ cup margarine   *½ cup honey*
½ cup peanut butter

Press together into balls or small candy-bar size and roll each in powdered sugar. Wrap each in aluminum foil and store in the freezer until you are ready to hit the trail. With nothing more than several bars of pemmican and water, you can spend days in the wilderness.

This fruit pemmican is loaded with energy, is tasty, keeps well, and is easy to prepare.

HARDTACK

3 cups unbleached white flour *1½ cups milk*
1½ cups graham flour   *1 teaspoon sugar*
½ cup shortening   *1 tablespoon salt*
½ cup cornmeal

Mix all ingredients together. Lightly grease and flour a 14″ × 16″ cookie sheet. Place an egg-sized piece of dough on the sheet. Roll it out with a sock-covered rolling pin until very thin. Bake the thin dough at 400°F until the edges are brown.

Flip the hardtack over and bake until cardboard stiff. Turn again and bake the other side cardboard stiff. Store in an airtight container. Serves 4.

PARCHED CORN

Buy frozen corn and set in sun until the corn is dry; this usually takes 1 day in a hot sun. Once you have dried corn, heat a large frying pan and add 1 tablespoon of vegetable cooking oil. Put in a cupful of dried corn, stir with a spoon, and shake the pan at the same time. When the corn kernels swell and turn a rich golden brown, they are done and should be removed since they burn easily. They should be stored in an airtight container. With a little practice you will be turning out parched corn that will rival that of any mountain person.

ROASTED PUMPKIN SEEDS

Remove stringy fiber that clings to pumpkin seeds. Spread seeds on a baking sheet and roast at 300°F for 15 to 20 minutes. Do not brown. Melt a little margarine in a skillet; add seeds and brown lightly, shaking pan constantly. Drain on absorbent paper towels and salt lightly. Pumpkin seeds are a good trail food.

ROASTED SOYBEANS

The superior protein content of soybeans is well known; their potential as a tasty and nutritious snack is less so, but is catching on.

Soak dried soybeans for 8 to 10 hours. Preheat oven to 350°F. Pat soybeans dry and spread on lightly oiled baking sheet. Cook until golden brown (about 1½ hours). If you like, sprinkle with salt or toss in soy sauce. To preserve freshness, store in airtight containers.

FRUIT LEATHER

Coat an 11″×16″ cookie sheet with non-grease spray or stick. Spread 4 cups of applesauce evenly on the sheet so that it is no more than ¼ inch thick. Dry the fruit puree in a slow oven (about 150°F) with the oven door slightly ajar for 6 to 8 hours. The door must be slightly open to allow the moisture to escape. When dry, the leather will be translucent, pliable, and barely sticky. Peel the fruit leather from the pan; roll and slice it into 8 small, individual rolls. Each roll of this pure fruit candy is the equivalent of ½ cup fruit. It makes a good school lunch treat as well as a trail snack.

Nuts and spices may be added to the puree for more flavor. The sliced rolls store well in large airtight jars.

BASIC GORP

1 cup cashews
1 cup raisins
1 cup shelled sunflower seeds

1 cup walnuts
1 cup M&M's candies

Mix together equal portions of cashews, raisins, walnuts, M&M's candies, and sunflower seeds. Package the mixture in individual plastic bags to be carried by each person.

GRANOLA

Commercial granola is often excellent but your own is usually better. The recipe that follows is a suggested framework around which you can concoct a mixture which best suits your own palate and energy requirements.

Mix together in a large bowl:

4½ cups rolled oats
1½ cups chopped walnuts
2 cups sunflower seeds

1 cup chopped dried fruit
½ cup shredded coconut
½ cup wheat germ

Add to dry mixture:

¾ cups honey
¼ cup sesame or sunflower oil

1 teaspoon salt
½ cup warm water

Mix well and spread on baking sheets. Bake in 275°F oven. Stir often until golden brown and continue to stir until cereal has cooled. Store in airtight containers. Makes about 12 cups.

OATCAKES

1 cup boiling water
½ teaspoon salt
1 tablespoon oil

3 cups oats
1 teaspoon cinnamon
2 tablespoons honey

Mix ingredients, stir, and leave for 20 minutes. Roll out batter to about ¼-inch thickness and cut into cakes. Brown both sides of cakes in unoiled skillet, then place in 200°F oven for ½ hour. When done, oatcakes will have the consistency of chocolate chip cookies. To keep them fresh, store in airtight containers. Serves 2.

MUESLI

You can eat this as is with milk and honey, or make it into a hot cereal by adding boiling water in proportions of 3 parts water to 1 part cereal mixture.

4 oz. (about 1½ cups) regular rolled oats
4 oz. crushed wheat
4 oz. crushed rye
4 oz. wheat germ
2 oz. raw, shelled sunflower seeds
2 oz. (about ¾ cup) shredded or grated coconut
2 oz. (about ½ cup) chopped nuts
1 teaspoon grated fresh orange or lemon peel

Shortly before the trip, mix all ingredients very well. Package in plastic bags. About 8 to 10 servings.

SURVIVAL BREAD

1 package (6 oz.) dates, chopped
1½ cups dark brown sugar,
*   firmly packed*
1 egg, beaten
1½ teaspoons baking soda

1¼ cups hot apricot or orange
*   juice*
6 tablespoons butter or
*   margarine*
2¼ cups sifted flour

1 cup chopped walnuts
1 small box candied cherries
1 square semi-sweet chocolate,
melted

1½ teaspoons salt
1½ cups seedless raisins
3 tablespoons wheat germ

Pour hot juice over chopped up dates and raisins, stir in sugar and butter, and let cool to room temperature.

Stir in beaten egg, walnuts, cherries, and melted chocolate.

Sift flour, soda, salt, and wheat germ and dump quickly into date mixture. Mix until just blended; pour into greased and waxed paper–lined loaf pan.

Let stand for 15 minutes and bake in moderate oven (350°F) for 1 hour or until center is firm. Test with toothpick. Cool on rack. This bread should be frozen and carried into the backcountry in an air-tight plastic bag. It should last slightly longer than commercial bread.

EXPEDITION MIX

1 lb. raisins or currants
1 lb. mixed dried fruits, chopped
½ lb. regular rolled oats
1 lb. wheat flakes
1 lb. rye flakes
½ lb. wheat germ

½ lb. shelled sunflower seeds
½ lb. sesame seeds
½ lb. soy lecithin
½ lb. shredded coconut
½ lb. chopped almonds and
walnuts (optional)

1½ tablespoons ground apple pie spice
(or about 3 teaspoons ground cinnamon,
1 teaspoon ground nutmeg, and
½ teaspoon ground cloves)
1½ teaspoons salt

Mix all ingredients thoroughly. Add 1½ teaspoons powdered milk per 4-oz. serving, package in plastic bags, and add water at eating time.

12

Making Your Own Dried Food

D rying is one of the oldest methods used to preserve food. For thousands of years, people have dried many foods to preserve them for trail use and use at home. The Indians throughout this continent were drying meat, fish, corn, squash, pumpkins, beans, and berries long before the Europeans ever arrived. Preservation of fresh vegetables and fruits by drying is still a great way to prepare your food for wilderness trips or for use at home. It is also interesting to note that drying is America's fastest growing method of food preserving. Drying preserves food by removing sufficient moisture to prevent its decay. Since drying reduces the size of the food, it has the advantage of conserving storage space as well. Water content of properly dried food is anywhere from 5 percent to 25 percent, reducing both weight and bulk.

As a youngster growing up in the southern Appalachians, I recall seeing strings of green beans hanging on the front porch walls of the remote mountaineers' cabins. The dried beans were called "leather britches" beans. I saw apple slices drying on the top of corn cribs and smokehouses. Pumpkins, peaches, sweet potatoes, corn, okra, and many other fruits and vegetables were sun dried for use in these mountain homesteads when money and transportation to town were both in short supply. I grew up eating these sun-dried foods and have always thought they were delicious.

Drying your own food can be a fun way to save energy while preparing wholesome, inexpensive, lightweight food. Drying foods at home can be accomplished several ways—in the sun as mentioned above, oven drying as discussed in the chapter on jerky, or drying in a commercial dehydrator.

SUN DRYING

Since I tend to lean towards the old ways of being self-sufficient, I like this method of drying foods best. It requires only energy from the sun, no chemicals or additives, and little equipment. All that is required is a sharp knife for cutting, a large piece of cheesecloth, screen wire or a fiberglass screen, a large pot, a drying rack, and some fresh fruit or vegetables.

The drying rack consists of the stand and the tray. The stand is simply something to sit the tray on. You can make a set of legs that looks like a table without a top, or you can use two sawhorses. The tray is a fine mesh screen. (An old window screen that you have cleaned will work well.) If you wish, you can make a permanent drying screen from a $4' \times 4'$ fiberglass screen and frame it as you would a window screen.

You can sun-dry fruits and vegetables at home for home and backcountry use.

The most important part of drying is air flow and temperature. Drying in the sun is unpredictable unless the drying tray temperature is over 100°F and the relative humidity is low. If the temperature is too low, humidity too high, or both, spoilage in the form of souring or molding will occur before drying is achieved.

Sun-Dried Fruit

Select ripe or overripe fruit such as apricots, apples, grapes, plums, berries, pineapples, oranges, pears, peaches, and tropical fruits.

Remove stones or pits from fruit. Seeds of berries or grapes need not be removed. Slice fruit about ¼ inch thick. Try to keep slices the same thickness for even drying. Spread on rack 1 layer thick and cover with cloth. The cloth covering keeps insects off the sweet-smelling fruit. The drying time will depend upon the type of fruit used and the temperature of the day. The process usually takes 1 or 2 days. If fruit takes more than 1 day, it is recommended that the racks be brought in at night out of the dew. Fruit is done when it feels leathery hard on the outside and a little bit soft on the inside.

Before storing fruit, first "test" it. Put it in a paper or cloth bag for a week. Stir it every day. You will know if the fruit is sufficiently dried and ready to store if no mold appears. For final storage put into airtight container, label, and date. Store in a dark, dry place.

Dried fruits can be eaten as they are, or they can be reconstituted by soaking in water overnight.

Sun-Dried Vegetables

Drying vegetables is more complicated than drying fruit. Select your vegetables carefully. If they are not fresh and are not in prime condition for cooking, they are not suitable for drying. Vegetables should be washed and prepared on the same day they are harvested, and they should be blanched (with steam) or parboiled a few minutes before drying. Blanching is the process of heating vegetables sufficiently to inactivate enzymes, the biological catalysts that facilitate chemical reactions in living tissue. If certain enzymes are not inactivated, they will cause color and flavor to deteriorate during drying and storage. Blanched vegetables, when dried, will have better flavor and color than unblanched ones. You may blanch with hot water or with steam. Water blanching usually results in more leaching of vegetable solids, but it takes less time than steam blanching under kitchen conditions.

With steam you need a kettle with a tightly fitting lid to use as a steaming container, and a colander, wire basket, or sieve that will fit into the kettle. Add 1½ to 2 inches of water to the steamer and heat to boiling. Place the colander, basket, or sieve containing loosely packed vegetables into the steamer and leave until the vegetables are heated through and wilted. See chart for recommended blanching times. Test by cutting through a piece of food. If sufficiently blanched, it should appear cooked (translucent) nearly to the center.

When blanching with water use only enough to cover the product. Bring the water to a boil and gradually stir in the vegetable, following the directions on the chart. Reuse the same water for additional lots when blanching the same vegetable, adding new water as necessary. Keep the lid on the saucepan while blanching.

After the heating process, cool quickly by rinsing in cold water; drain well. Spread cut or diced vegetables on trays leaving air spaces. Turn or stir every 3 or 4 hours. Most vegetables take from 1 to 3 days, depending upon the heat of the day. Remember to bring trays in at night. Check vegetables the same as you would fruit; they should be a little bit more brittle than fruit. Storing for both is the same.

The leather britches beans I mentioned earlier may be dried by stringing the tender green beans this way:

1. Thread a long needle with a long, strong thread and tie a large knot at the end.
2. Push the needle through the center of each green bean.
3. Continue threading beans, pushing them together at the end of the thread.
4. Hang one end of the threaded beans from a nail in a warm, airy place but not in direct sunlight.
5. Let hang until beans are dry.
6. Store in cloth bag until ready to use.

To reconstitute dried vegetables, water removed during drying must be replaced either by soaking, cooking, or a combination of both. Root, stem, and seed vegetables should be soaked for ½ to 2 hours in sufficient cold water to keep them covered. After soaking, simmer until tender, allowing excess water to evaporate.

Greens, cabbages, and tomatoes do not need to be soaked. Simply add sufficient water to keep them covered, and simmer until tender.

OVEN DRYING

For oven drying meat, see the chapter on jerky.

OVEN-DRIED FRUITS

Prepare fruit as for sun drying. Set oven at lowest setting. Place the fruit on cookie sheets and put in oven, leaving the oven door open approximately 2 inches. The fruit will dry in 4 to 5 hours. Store as discussed in sun drying.

OVEN-DRIED VEGETABLES

Select, blanch, and slice as for sun drying. Next, follow these steps:

1. Load 2 to 4 cookie trays with no more than 4 to 6 lbs. of prepared vegetables distributed among them. Vegetable pieces should be in a single layer with 3 inches of free space at the top of the oven. More than 1 kind of vegetable can be dried at the same time. Strong-smelling vegetables should be dried separately.
2. Place an accurate and easily read thermometer on the top tray toward the back.
3. Preheat the oven to 160°F and then add the loaded trays. Prop the door open at least 4 inches.
4. Place a fan outside the oven in such a position that air is directed through the opening and across the oven. Change the position of the fan frequently during drying to vary the circulation of air.
5. Maintain the temperature at 140°F. It takes less heat to keep the temperature at 140°F as drying progresses, so watch the temperature carefully toward the end of the drying.
6. Examine the vegetables often, and turn the trays frequently. At the start of the drying process there is little danger of scorching, but when nearly dry the vegetables may scorch

easily. Even slight scorching destroys the flavor and may lower the nutritive value, so be careful not to allow the temperature to rise above 140°F, especially during the latter stages of drying.

7. Consult the chart for the correct drying periods. Store and reconstitute as instructed in sun drying.

COMMERCIAL DEHYDRATORS

If you really become interested in drying fruits and vegetables, consider a commercial dehydrator. (For address, see list of suppliers in the back of this book.) These electrical, fan-blown units are excellent for home use where electricity is available. The one that I am most familiar with is the Excalibur Dehydrator, which has models offering four-, five-, and nine-tray drying capacities.

This brand dries food at gentle, low temperatures (85°F to 145°F), and all the trays are equally exposed to the warm circulating air because of the horizontal air-flow system. Rotation of the trays is not necessary.

Complete instructions and recipes come with each unit.

Regardless of which method you choose, drying is one of the best ways to make your own lightweight backcountry food or to preserve food for home use.

HOME DRYING OF VEGETABLES

Vegetables	Preparation	Blanching		Drying	
		Method	Time Minutes	Method	Time Hours
Beans, Green	Wash thoroughly, cut in short pieces or lengthwise.	Steam Water	2–2½ 2	Oven Sun	3–6 8
Beets	Cook as usual. Cool, peel. Cut into shoe-string strips ⅛ inch thick.	Already cooked: no further blanching		Oven Sun	3–5 8–10
Broccoli	Trim, cut as for serving. Wash thoroughly. Quarter stalks lengthwise.	Steam Water*	3–3½ 2	Oven Sun	3–4½ 8–10
Cabbage	Remove outer leaves, quarter, and core. Cut into strips, ⅛ inch thick.	Steam until wilted. Water	2½–3 1½–2	Oven Sun	1–3 6–7
Carrots	Use only crisp, tender carrots. Wash thoroughly. Cut off roots and tops. Preferably peel, cut in slices or strips, ⅛ inch thick.	Steam Water	4–5 3½	Oven Sun	3½–5 8
Cauliflower	Prepare as for serving.	Steam Water*	4–5 3–4	Oven Sun	4–6 8–11
Celery	Trim stalks; wash and slice stalks.	Steam Water	2 2	Oven Sun	3–4 8
Corn-on-the-Cob	Husk, trim.	Steam until milk does not exude from kernel when cut. Water	1½	Oven Sun	4–6 8

continued

		Blanching		Drying	
			Time		Time
Vegetables	Preparation	Method	Minutes	Method	Hours
Corn, cut	Prepare in same manner as corn-on-the-cob, except cut kernels from cob after blanching.			Oven Sun	2–3 6
Eggplant	Use same directions as for summer squash.	Steam Water	3½ 3	Oven Sun	3½–5 6–8
Okra	Wash, trim and slice crosswise in ⅛–¼-inch disks.	None		Oven Sun	4–6 8–11
Onions	Wash, remove outer paper shells. Remove tops and root ends. Slice ⅛–¼-inch thick.	None		Oven Sun	3–6 8–11
Peas	Shell.	Steam Water	3 2	Oven Sun	3 6–8
Peppers and Pimentos	Wash, stem and core. Remove partitions. Cut into disks, ⅜ by ⅜ inch.	None	—	Oven Sun	2½–5 6–8
Potatoes	Wash, peel and cut into shoe-string strips ¼-inch thick, or cut into slices ⅛-inch thick.	Steam Water	6–8 5–6	Oven Sun	4–6 8–11
Spinach and other Greens (Kale, Chard, Mustard)	Trim and wash very thoroughly.	Steam until thoroughly wilted. Water	2–2½ 1½	Oven Sun	2½–3½ 6–8
Squash, Banana	Wash, peel and slice in strips about ¼-inch thick.	Steam Water	2½–3 1	Oven Sun	4–5 6–8
Squash, Summer	Wash, trim and cut into ¼-inch slices.	Steam Water	2½–3 1½	Oven Sun	4–6 6–8
Tomatoes for Stewing	Steam or dip in boiling water to loosen skins. Chill in cold water. Peel; cut into sections ¾-inch wide or slice. Cut small pear or plum tomatoes in half.	Steam Water	3 1	Oven Sun	6–8 8–10

*Preferred Method

CHAPTER 13

Smoking Food

There was once a time when, if people needed food for the kitchen, they ran out past the well in the backyard to the smokehouse. Here the fruits of the family's labor were stored. The smokehouse was the pride and joy of the farm. In it, cured venison quarters hung from the rafters and, on a shelf in the back, hams were curing in salt. The smokehouse smelled of hickory, permeating the foods it held with a smoky taste everyone enjoyed.

The days of the smokehouse are all but gone; however, people can still enjoy home-smoked foods on the patio or in camp. Today a rapidly growing interest in smoking foods has given rise to several new products that enable anyone to smoke favorite meats, seafood, and fishes. These new smokers operate either on charcoal or electrical elements. Many are equipped with a water pan that sits just under the food ensuring moist, juicy, smoke cooking. When selected wood chips are added to the charcoal or placed on a pan above the electrical element, a delicious variety of smoking effects takes place.

THE COMMERCIAL SMOKER

The smoker I have come to trust is the charcoal-gas-fired Master-Built 7-in-1 made by the MasterBuilt Mfg. Corp. of Columbus, Georgia. (For complete ordering address, see list of suppliers in the back of this book.)

The secret of the smoker is the long, slow, even cooking. The water pan between the food and the flames holds the temperature low and even and acts as an automatic baster.

Cooking on the smoker should not be rushed; it takes several hours. But unlike most methods of cooking, you do not have to be around all these hours. Once the food is in the smoker you can go fishing or visit with a neighbor. Tom Gresham, a good friend and fellow outdoor writer, calls his smoker his "backyard crock pot." He says when he is working on a magazine article he takes a break at lunch, fires up his smoker, places the food in it, and goes back to work. Come dinner time he has a tasty meal ready to eat. Food seldom overcooks in a smoker if the instructions are properly followed. The low temperatures hold the food at the proper doneness.

The mouth-watering goodness of smoke-cooked foods comes from the aromatic wood used to make the smoke. Woods such as aspen, alder, oak, maple, walnut, hickory, apple, cherry, peach, or mesquite are excellent. I prefer fruitwoods, but I have enjoyed excellent meals using oak. I am told that down in Florida smoking fans use palmetto and mangrove. I also know of a man in Iowa who uses dried corn-cobs to create excellent table fare. You *do not* want to use resinous soft-woods such as pine or cedar. These will make your foods taste like they were marinated in turpentine.

The days of the smoke house are nearly gone, but good smoked foods may be prepared on the patio or in camp using the modern smoker.

Green wood, perhaps twigs from an apple or hickory tree, makes a very dense smoke that heavily flavors food. A three- to four-inch stick or several small twigs will be enough for a full fire pan.

There are several rules to follow in order to get the most out of a smoker.

- Do not peek at the food while cooking. It is hard to resist, but each time you lift the cover heat and moisture escape, and that slows cooking down. If you cannot help yourself, add at least fifteen minutes cooking time for each time you peek. It is wiser to be patient and check only at the end of the recommended cooking time.
- Be sure that food to be smoked is completely thawed. Also, let food stand at room temperature while building the fire and soaking the wood so that it is not cold when it goes onto the grill.
- Several factors affect cooking time: outside temperature, wind, altitude, temperature of food as it goes in the unit, and quality of charcoal used. Always add at least another hour of cooking time if the outdoor temperature is below 55°F, even more time if it is colder than that. More charcoal will also be needed.
- You can cook vegetables right along with the main course in a smoker. Most vegetables take four to five hours. If you do not want smoky tasting vegetables, simply wrap them in aluminum foil before putting them in the smoker.

Smoked Nuts

Make a shallow tray of heavy-duty aluminum foil to fit on cooking grill. Spread whole plain or salted almonds, walnuts, filberts, pecans, or peanuts on foil tray. Smoke for several hours. Cool, then store in tightly covered containers or plastic bags. Great for appetizers, nibblers, or with fruit for dessert.

Smoked Cheese

Use an 8-oz. package of cream cheese, or any other cheese such as Monterey jack, Muenster, or cheddar. Cheese should be a fairly flat rectangle, shaped much like the cream cheese, and not more than about 1 inch thick. Put several pieces of cheese on a piece of foil and put on cooking grill. Cover and smoke for 1 or 2 hours. Take cheese out if it begins to melt. Serve while warm to spread on crackers for appetizers or with fruit for dessert; or cool, then wrap well and chill until ready to serve.

SMOKED SALT

For smoked salt to use in seasoning jerky, make a shallow tray of heavy duty aluminum foil to fit in center of cooking grill. Spread a very shallow layer of table salt on foil tray. Cover and smoke several hours or until salt is slightly colored and tastes smoky. Cool and store in tightly covered container. Can be used in cooking to add smoke flavor or as a table seasoning.

DUCK À L'ORANGE

1 (4–5 lb.) duckling
1 cup orange juice
1 onion, quartered
1 apple, quartered
1 teaspoon garlic, onion, or celery salt

1 tablespoon grated orange peel
3 stalks celery, including leaves, sliced
1 cup wine

Put duckling in large heavy duty plastic bag or deep bowl. (Turkey or chicken may be substituted.) Combine orange juice and peel, wine, and salt and pour over duckling. Close bag or cover bowl, and refrigerate several hours or overnight, turning duckling in marinade occasionally. Lift duckling from marinade, put onion, apple, and celery into cavity, and put on cooking grill. Pour marinade into water pan. Smoke about 6 to 8 hours or until leg can be moved easily in joint. Use juices in water pan for sauce. Serves 6.

SMOKED FISH

1 quart water
1 tablespoon dried tarragon leaves (optional)
2 to 3 lbs. fresh (thawed) fish fillets, steaks, or small, whole dressed fish

¼ cup salt

Mix water and salt until salt dissolves. Pour into large glass baking dish or other shallow container. Arrange fish fillets, steaks, or whole butterflied fish in brine; cover and refrigerate several hours or overnight. Before starting fire or preparing smoker, lift fish from brine and arrange on wire racks to air dry for twenty to thirty minutes. Be sure to grease cooking grill or spray with pan coating. Arrange fish in a single layer on cooking grill, leaving space between pieces if possible. Add tarragon to ⅔ full water pan. Smoke about 2 to 3 hours over charcoal, 1½ to 2½ hours for electric, or until fish flakes with a fork.

SMOKED OYSTERS

Arrange oysters on well-buttered foil tray. The oysters should be brushed with a mixture of melted butter and lemon juice. Put in smoker and cook about 1 to 2 hours or until firm.

THE IMPROVISED SMOKER

Several years ago while fishing in the Yukon, I learned how Indians improvise a smoker when they want to preserve fish. This smoker is quick to make and does a good job when properly attended. Here is how my Cree Indian guide taught me to make the smoker.

1. Obtain three poles, each eight feet long, and lash them together at one end. Spread the opposite ends outward to form a three-legged tepee frame.
2. Lash a "fish-hanging" stick between each of the tepee legs, approximately four feet above the ground. A strong cord tied between the legs will also work.
3. Cover the tepee frame with a tarp, heavy plastic, or, as I saw one fisherman use, a rescue blanket. Leave an opening at the tepee top for smoke to exit and make sure the bottom is left off the ground so that air will be fed into the tepee.
4. Start a very small fire in the center of the tepee with small pieces of dry wood, then add green hardwood or water-soaked hardwood chips. Keep the fire small and smoky so the fish will not cook and you will not burn your tepee cover.
5. Maintain a steady smoke for approximately twelve hours.

In order to prepare fish for the improvised smoker, fillet the fish as you usually would except leave the fillets attached to the tail. This allows you to hang the two fillets, still attached, over the hanging stick or cord in the tepee. Next, dry the fillets with a towel and rub the dry fish with salt. Many guides use seasoning salt, and I admit that I like it better than plain salt. After salting hang the fillets to air cure for four hours. When you are ready to hang the fillets in the smoker, make five or six shallow cuts across the width of the fillet to expose more surfaces to the smoke. Smoke the fillets for twelve hours. Store in a porous sack and be sure the smoked fillets are kept dry.

SMOKED SALMON

20 lbs. salmon (or any saltwater fish)	*1 lb. salt*
	1 oz. crushed bay leaves
1 oz. cloves	*1 oz. mace*
2 lbs. fine grain salt	*1 oz. white pepper*
1 gallon water	*2 lbs. brown sugar*

In my opinion, there are few foods on earth better than smoked salmon. Any time I get a chance to go salmon fishing along the Pacific coast I try to smoke a good supply of these delicious fish. Here is the way Pete Murray, a fisheries biologist with the Alaska Department of Fish and Game, smokes his salmon.

First, clean, slime, and fillet the fish, after rigor mortis has set in. At this stage, the flesh will be firm, making it easier to separate from the bones. For convenience in hanging, the tail should be left intact with each fillet. Then soak the fish in a salt brine consisting of 2 lbs. fine grain salt to 1 gallon of water for 1 hour. When removed from this solution, permit fillets to air dry 15 to 20 minutes.

Next, rub a sugar and spice mixture consisting of the brown sugar, salt, bay leaves, cloves, mace, and white pepper thoroughly into the flesh. For good penetration, sprinkle a thin layer of the remaining mixture into the bottom of a plastic container and cover with a single row of fish, skin side down. Place another layer of the mixture between the flesh and the upper side of the fillets, and so on, until all of the fish has been covered. This mixture should be enough to cure 20 lbs. of fish. Allow to sit for 10 hours.

Next, thoroughly wash each fish to remove most of the spices, and air dry 4 to 6 hours. If the humidity is high, a fan may be used to facilitate drying. It is important to make certain a glaze has formed on the fillets before smoke curing, because excess moisture and heat may cause the meat to soften and fall from the stringer. After fish are glazed by air drying, place the fillets in an improvised smoker or, if you are lucky enough to know someone with one, in a smokehouse, and cure at 85°F for 8 to 10 hours. Mild cures of this nature must either be consumed immediately, quick frozen, or canned.

To ensure preservation and quality, canning is recommended. Steam exhaust or vacuum seal the fish and process for 75 minutes at 240°F (10 lbs. pressure). A tablespoon of salad oil may be added to each ½ lb. can of fish to supplement natural oils. Take care not to over smoke cure, as canning and storage will enhance the smoke flavor of fish.

If a hard cure is desired, continue smoke curing the fish at 85°F for 5 to 6 days or to taste. Brush the finished product with salad oil and store under refrigeration for long preservation.

CHAPTER 14

Cooking with Charcoal

O ne of the most pleasant methods of cooking is over charcoal. This simple cooking technique is a favorite of millions of Americans both at home on the patio and in the outdoors on picnics and camping trips.

Charcoal grills come in many sizes, shapes, and patterns. Some are simply wire grills that rest on two rocks with a bed of coals on the ground between them. Then there is the permanent fire pit, made from stones or bricks overlaid with a mesh grill. These pits are usually found in campgrounds, picnic areas, and backyards. The most common grill is the pressed metal grill or brazier that enables one to adjust the height of the grill above the coals. The better models will have a hood that serves as a heat reflector, and vent openings that allow the heat to be adjusted.

Cooking tools for charcoal grilling are inexpensive and few. You will need two sets of long tongs, one set for food and one set for coals. Tongs are much better for turning meat than a fork. The tines of a fork stick into the meat and release its juices, thus robbing it of flavor. You will also need a long-handled basting brush and a long-handled spoon. All should have wooden handles to protect your hands.

In addition to these cooking tools, you will need a grill scraper (I use a wire welder's brush), a small toy shovel, a box of kitchen matches, mitten-shaped pot holders, and a pump spray bottle filled with water.

Use care in deciding where to place the grill. I know of a fellow who set his garage ceiling on fire; another set the woods around his camp on fire; and another tipped his coals onto the deck of his house boat. Place the grill away from any combustibles, buildings,

Charcoal is an American tradition. *Photo courtesy of the Aluminum Association.*

dry grass or leaves, or bushes. Keep it out of the wind if possible—or at least away from where people are sitting so that a gust of wind will not blow smoke and sparks on them. On windy days, a grill windshield helps control fire. Check that the grill is stable and that it is out of the path of running children or the adults' walkway. Always use your grill in a well-ventilated area, not in a garage, tent, recreational vehicle, or boat. There is danger from both fumes and fire; burning charcoal gives off carbon monoxide, which can be fatal if inhaled.

If you are going to use commercial charcoal, be sure you get a quality product; it may cost a little more but is well worth the price. Most high-quality charcoal briquettes are pillow shaped. They burn evenly with no smoke or odor and last longer in actual use than lump charcoal. The cheaper lump charcoal is uneven in size and can produce uneven heat, smoke, and often sparks. The pillow-shaped briquettes light easily and quickly, radiating cooking heat in about a half-hour.

You can make your own charcoal if you have a supply of hardwood. Simply build a fire and let it burn down to a bed of hot coals. The coals can be transferred to a grill with a shovel, or they can be drowned out with water, dried, and saved for future use.

Before placing charcoal in the grill, you may want to increase the efficiency of your grill by lining it with heavy duty aluminum foil. The fire may be built directly on the foil. Fine stones or gravel may be placed on the foil and the fire built on top. This will create a good draft for the fire. Some grills have a grate for holding the fire; in this case, line the ash pit. Foil reflects the heat back onto the food, and speeds up cooking too. It helps keep the grill clean by catching melted fat and drippings. When cooking is finished and the fire dead, throw foil with remaining ashes into the trash can.

To save partially burned briquettes for another use, close foil tightly over the fire and smother it. Protect hands with mitts. If you are using a grill without a hood and the day is windy, use extra long lengths of foil to line the grill. Bring the foil up and partially over to shield the food and to hold in the heat.

The simplest way to get the fire going is to use an electric starter (assuming there is an electric outlet nearby). Place the starter on the charcoal; the gray ash (which indicates the charcoal is burning) will develop in minutes.

A great way to speed up fire starting is to light the charcoal in a metal container such as a coffee can. Remove both ends of the can and punch holes in the sides around the bottom with a can opener. Place the can in a fire bowl, fill with charcoal, sprinkle in starter fluid, and light. When the charcoal is ready, remove the can and add the rest of the charcoal.

If using a liquid starter, place the charcoal in a pyramid in the center of the firebox and drizzle the starter over the charcoal. Let it stand for a few minutes to soak up the fluid, then light in several places with long kitchen matches.

Solid and semisolid starter and ready-to-start packages of briquettes are more expensive, but are good for outings since there is no danger of flammable fluid being spilled.

After the fire is going, wait approximately twenty minutes or until two-thirds of the charcoal is covered with gray ash before cooking. Spread the ash-covered charcoal around the grill in the pattern needed for the particular kind of grilling. It will take a total of about thirty minutes before the charcoal reaches the right temperature.

The biggest mistakes made by novice outdoor cooks are using too much charcoal and making too large a fire. A single layer of charcoal is all that is necessary.

Caution: *Never* use kerosene or gasoline to start a fire or you may become a human torch. *Never* add more liquid starter once the charcoal has ignited because it can flare up dramatically. Also, be sure to wear clothes without dangling shirttails, sleeves, strings, or any other pieces that can inadvertently stray too close to a flame. More than one charcoal chef has caught on fire by wearing loose clothing.

Once the coals are ready, use tongs to spread them out evenly in the grill. If you plan to grill for more than thirty minutes, place a dozen new briquettes around the outer edge of the hot coals, moving them into the center when gray.

Brush the grill rack with fat or oil just before cooking to prevent food from sticking.

There are two ways to test the temperature of your coals. One method is to use a disk-like thermometer made for charcoal grills. The other method is simple and requires only your hand. Hold your hand palm-side down just above the grill surface for as long as you can. Two or three seconds means the temperature is hot, over 375°F; four seconds is warm, over 300°F; five to six seconds is low, over 200°F.

If the fire is too hot, separate the coals, raise the grill rack, or close the vent openings. To increase heat during cooking, open the vents, tap the ashes off the charcoal, or lower the grill rack closer to the fire.

To stop flare-ups, raise the grill rack and space coals farther apart. If this does not work, move the food to one side to prevent ashes from getting on the food, and spray the coals with water. Be careful not to overdo it or you might lose your heat. One of the chief causes of flare-ups is meat that still has a thick layer of fat attached. Trim most of the fat off cuts of meat before grilling.

You can save used charcoal for another cookout by removing the coals with tongs, placing them in a metal bucket, and covering to smother. Many hood-type grills allow you to smother the coals simply by closing the vents and lowering the hood. You can also put out hot coals with water and, when dry, use them again.

To prolong the life of your grill, it is important to keep it clean. Place the grill rack on just before cooking and remove after the cooking is complete. Clean as soon as possible by washing in soapy water with a stiff brush.

If you use small rocks as a grill base, wash them in hot water after several uses.

To store your grill for long periods of time, clean thoroughly, oil the rack lightly with vegetable oil, and cover well.

One of the major problems I hear about with charcoal grill cooking is hamburgers that fall apart and slip down into the fire. To make a hamburger that will hold together while cooking, add one egg and one-fourth cup of breadcrumbs to each pound of meat. You can also cook hamburgers on foil. Punch holes in the foil at one-inch intervals to let the fat drip down into the fire and the smoke flavor the meat.

Here are other charcoal grill favorites.

Fish and game may be prepared in camp on a charcoal grill.

GRILLED TURKEY

For a turkey that is roasted to a rich, ruddy-brown color, with crisp and succulent skin, moist meat, and more flavor than any you have tasted before, try roasting this wonderful bird on an outdoor barbecue grill.

You will need a grill with a domed hood to close over the turkey. The heat will be reflected down onto the bird, making an oven out of the grill.

The grill should be at least 24 inches in diameter if the round brazier type. If rectangular in shape, it should be about 14 inches wide by about 24 inches long. These sizes will accommodate turkeys up to 14 lbs. purchased ready-to-cook weight.

1. Set up the grill where it is out of the wind.
2. Build a fire at one end of the grill using about half a 5-lb. bag of charcoal briquettes. At the other end place a shallow foil-lined pan.
3. Place the grate in position over the charcoal, and, when the fire is burning enough to create considerable heat, place the turkey on the grate over the pan—not over the fire. The turkey should be stuffed and trussed in the usual way.
4. Cover, or place a foil hood on the grill, adjusting the damper so the fire will burn moderately. Do not try to rush the roasting. Brush the turkey once or twice with melted shortening or a basting sauce of wine or cider and herbs. Should the side of the turkey closest to the fire tend to brown too quickly, protect it with foil. Add additional briquettes once or twice during the roasting and a few damp hickory chips towards the end.
5. Roast the turkey about the same length of time as for oven roasting. A 14-lb. turkey should take about 4 hours. The usual tests for doneness can be used—the drumstick and thigh joint should move easily, and the breast should feel soft when pressed with your fingers. An oven thermometer inserted into the thickest part of the thigh should read 185°F.

Drippings in the foil-lined pan will make terrific gravy. A 14-lb. turkey serves 12.

BEER BURGERS

This is a great way to keep hamburgers warm when cooking for a crowd. Makes 12 hamburgers.

3 lbs. ground beef
1 teaspoon salt
½ teaspoon pepper
½ cup (1 stick) butter or
margarine

1 can (12 oz.) beer
¼ teaspoon salt
dash liquid hot
pepper seasoning

Mix meat lightly with 1 teaspoon salt and the pepper and shape into patties.

Melt butter in shallow baking pan on grill; add beer, ¼ teaspoon salt, and hot pepper sauce.

Grill hamburgers about 5 inches from the coals to desired degree of doneness, about 5 minutes on one side and 3 minutes on the other for medium rare. As hamburgers cook, place them in beer mixture to keep warm until all are cooked.

Note: any extra beer mixture will add a special flavor to pot roast or stews. Boil mixture 5 minutes, cool, and refrigerate until ready to reuse.

SKEWERED BEEF BALLS

1 lb. ground beef
2 tablespoons fine dry bread
crumbs
prepared mustard
12 frankfurter buns, toasted
1 egg

18 slices bacon (about 1 lb.)
6 frankfurters
1 tablespoon Worcestershire
sauce
1 teaspoon garlic salt

Combine ground beef, bread crumbs, Worcestershire sauce, egg, and garlic salt. Form mixture into 12 meatballs and place 1 meatball onto each of 6 skewers. Partially cook bacon on grill. Cut each frankfurter into 4 pieces. Wrap a slice of bacon around 2 frankfurter pieces; arrange on skewers, fastening ends of bacon together. Form each of 6 slices of bacon into an S shape; arrange on skewers and add final meatball to each. Grill over coals until done. Spread the mixed grill with mustard and serve on toasted buns. Makes 12 sandwiches.

CAMPHOUSE ROAST BEEF

3 to 4 lbs. beef pot roast *4 to 6 carrots, cut lengthwise*
1 envelope chili seasoning *2 tomatoes, sliced*
2 onions, sliced

Coat pot roast with contents of chili seasoning envelope. Place meat on 2 large sheets of heavy duty aluminum foil. Top with onion and tomato slices; arrange carrots around sides of roast. Wrap securely, using double folds. Place on grill; cook over hot coals 1¼ hours. Replenish fire if necessary. Turn package and cook an additional 45 minutes or until meat is tender. Makes 6 to 8 servings.

GRILLED PORK CHOPS

4 to 6 pork shoulder chops *¼ cup bottled salad dressing*
1 envelope brown gravy mix *(any flavor)*
sliced dill pickles, sliced raw *½ cup water*
carrots, or sliced onions

Place each pork chop on a 10-inch square of heavy-duty aluminum foil. Stir together contents of gravy mix envelope, water, and salad dressing; spoon some of mixture onto each chop and top with a few slices of pickle, carrot, or onion. Wrap tightly. Grill about 4 inches above hot coals for 30 to 40 minutes, turning frequently, until tender and well cooked. Serves 4 to 6.

GRILLED FISH FILLETS

2 lbs. fish fillets *½ cup mayonnaise*
salad oil or butter *2 tablespoons lemon juice*
1 envelope seasoning mix for *sliced tomatoes and pickle*
sloppy joes *relish*

Cut 4 to 6 lengths of heavy duty aluminum foil; generously grease 1 side of each with oil or butter. Place a serving size piece of fish on each length of foil. Stir together contents of seasoning mix envelope, mayonnaise, and lemon juice; spread over both sides of fish. Place a tomato slice and a spoonful of relish on each. Wrap foil around fish, sealing edges with a tight double fold. Place on grill 3 to 4 inches above hot coals. Cook 10 to 20 minutes, turning once, until fish flakes easily when pierced with a fork. Serves 4 to 6.

CHICKEN DINNERS IN A PACKAGE

1 fryer	*pepper*
onion	*dill*
zucchini, summer squash, or	*water*
snap beans	*salt*
butter	

Purchase chicken cut as for frying, with legs and second joints separated, etc. Remove as many broken or protruding bones as possible. Rinse and pat dry with paper towel. Place a sufficient piece for 1 serving in center of each large square of heavy duty aluminum foil. Add 1 or 2 small onion slices and several slices of zucchini, summer squash, or snap beans. Season with salt, pepper, and a little dill. Then add 1 tablespoon water and a pat of butter to each. Bring foil up over chicken and seal edges together with a tight double fold. Seal ends in same manner to make a tight package. Place on grill over moderately hot fire and cook, turning once or twice, for about 50 minutes or until done.

Chicken will brown through the foil and a delicious gravy will form as the flavors mix during the cooking process. These chicken dinners can be eaten right from the foil package.

CHAPTER 15

Bean Hole Cooking

A favorite method of cooking in hunting and fishing camps in northeastern U. S. and Canada is what is commonly called "bean hole cooking." Dating back to early colonial days, this method of baking in a hole in the ground has survived several hundred years of improvements in ovens and baking techniques. Back before electric and gas stoves were common, logging camp cooks, remote resort lodge cooks, hunting and fishing camp cooks, and homestead cooks did much of their baking in cast iron Dutch ovens in a hole filled with hot coals and covered with dirt. Because beans were the most common dish baked, this technique was named "bean hole cooking."

Each year I hunt and fish with Pam and Ken French from their log-cabin camp, named Camp Quitchabitchin, in central Maine. Outside their cabin, down near the lake shore, Ken has built a permanent bean hole. Miss Pam prepares her tasty dishes that require baking and Ken places the cast iron pot into the hot coals in the bean hole. The top is placed on the hole and it is covered with dirt. After a day of hunting or fishing, we return, uncover the pot or pots, and the evening meal is hot and ready to eat.

Following Ken's instruction, I have built a permanent bean hole at my cabin in Cross Creek Hollow in Alabama. Now it is the center of attention anytime I am cooking for a group of guests. Here is how you can build your own permanent bean hole.

Take a clean 55-gallon drum and cut it in half. Save the lid and discard the upper half. In a safe area, outside your cabin or camp, dig a hole a little deeper and wider than the half drum. Line the bottom and side of the hole with firebricks. Next, drill several small holes in the bottom of the drum to allow water to drain in the event it should ever get inside. Place about three inches of sand in the bottom of the drum to prevent it from burning out. Put the drum in the firebrick-lined hole and fill in the spaces between the bricks, and between the bricks and drum, with sand. Place the lid on top of the drum and you have a permanent bean hole.

When you want to bake a pot of beans—or any other dish— simply build a fire in a nearby fire pit and when a hot bed of coals is ready take a shovel and transfer them into the bean hole. Leave the top off and let the hole get hot. Next place a cast iron Dutch oven filled with beans into the bed of coals in the bean hole, put a couple of shovels of hot coals on top of the Dutch oven. Put the cover on top of the drum and cover with dirt or sand. This will keep the temperature even for a long period of time. Go hiking or fishing for the day and return to a hot meal. As with most methods of cooking, it will take a few trials to get the method perfected, but it is fun and, once it is worked out, will become a favorite method of baking in your camp.

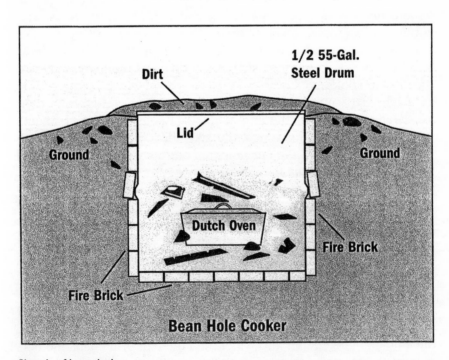

Sketch of bean hole.

The permanent bean hole is easy to use and make.

Covering the bean hole with soil seals in the heat to use in baking.

Here is Miss Pam's recipe for her famous bean hole beans.

BEAN HOLE BEANS

2 lbs. Dry Red Kidney beans   *2 medium onions*
½ lb. Bacon (cut into pieces)   *2 Tsp. Dry Mustard*
¾ cups Molasses   *Salt and Pepper*
1¾ cups Brown Sugar

Soak beans in water for approximately 12 hours before putting them in cast iron Dutch oven. Do not drain beans, bring beans to a boil and stir in all above ingredients. Stir Well.

Cover oven with aluminum foil, place the cover on the foil, and cover tightly with aluminum foil again. Bury in coals and cook approximately 15 hours.

16

Making Water Safe for Drinking

There once was a time when it would have been unnecessary to include a chapter in this book on how to make water safe for drinking, but I am afraid that those days have gone the way of the passenger pigeon and the mountain man. Today there are few areas left in the wilderness or anywhere else where one can trust the quality of the water and be safe in doing so. Therefore, it behooves every backcountry traveler to learn the skill of making water safe for drinking.

Most people who go into the backcountry are involved in vigorous activities such as hunting, fishing, or backpacking, and pure drinking water is essential. The body is approximately 75 percent water, and the intake and output of liquids are necessary for normal functions of the vital organs.

Daily water requirements, a minimum of two quarts, help maintain proper balance and efficiency within the system of the body. During cold weather breathing alone releases a lot of moisture from the body. Perspiration also releases moisture. Any lower intake of water results in gradual dehydration and the loss of the body's efficiency. Losing water to the extent of 2.5 percent of body weight, or approximately one and one-half quarts of body water, will reduce efficiency 25 percent. This loss could be deadly in the wilderness.

There are many myths about water purifying itself in the outdoors. One popular theory is that water, swiftly running over, around, and through rocks purifies itself. Do not believe it. This is not a valid hypothesis. Another myth claims that if clear water sits in the sun for an hour the germs are killed. Again, this is untrue. Nature produces clean water, but once it becomes unclean, rarely does nature reclean it. It is your responsibility to treat questionable water.

Never trust water from an unknown source. Once I was trout fishing with a friend in a western state. The stream we were wading through looked crystal clear and, on the surface, appeared to flow from a wilderness. We stopped for a lunch break near another fisherman and started to bend down to drink the water. "Hold it," the stranger shouted. We stopped as he walked over to where we were standing. "This stream runs through a ski area and a cabin complex about two miles upstream," he told us. "There is raw sewage seeping into this very stream up there." Then he offered us water from his canteen, which we gladly accepted. If you do not know the source of your water supply, do not trust it.

Some of the diseases you may contract by drinking impure water include dysentery, giardia, cholera, and typhoid.

The best way to be assured of having safe water is to carry enough with you to use for drinking and cooking. However, on backpacking trips and other expeditions of several days, this is not always possible. It is on these types of trips that water treatment knowledge is a must.

Here are several methods for treating questionable water.

BOILING WATER

One of the best methods for treating water is the boiling method. Boiling water for ten minutes will produce germ-free water for drinking or cooking. Since boiling leaves water with a flat taste, you should pour it back and forth between two containers several times once it has cooled. This aerates it, restoring its natural taste. I have found that my backpack stove comes in handy for boiling water. It is also a common practice in Rocky Mountain camps to keep a large coffee-pot of boiling water on the back of the sheepherder's stove. There is always a need for more safe water.

CLOROX TREATMENT

Clorox, the washing bleach that makes clothes sparkling white, is another excellent water treatment. To each quart of questionable water, add ten drops of pure Clorox. If for some reason the water is cloudy, add twenty drops. Next, shake the water vigorously, then let it sit for thirty minutes. There should be a slight chlorine odor and taste if the water is properly treated. If not, add another ten drops of Clorox and let the water stand for an additional fifteen minutes.

COMMERCIAL TABLETS

Drug stores and outfitter stores usually have halazone tablets or Potable-Aqua tablets for the treatment of water. Both do an excellent job. Halazone tablets have been used successfully for years. Add two tablets to a quart of water and follow with a thirty-minute wait. The newer product, Potable-Aqua, requires one tablet to a quart of water, capping loosely to allow a little leakage. Wait three minutes and shake thoroughly. Wait ten minutes before drinking. If the water is very cold or contains rotten leaves or silt, use two tablets and wait twenty minutes before drinking.

IODINE TREATMENT

While iodine is no longer used in some of the newer first-aid kits, it is still in older kits and makes a good water treatment. Simply add five drops of iodine to one quart of clear water and ten drops to cloudy water. Let water stand for thirty minutes before drinking.

At this point I should mention that any time you are treating water in a canteen, jug, or other type of container, you should be sure to rinse the cap, spout, screw threads, lid, and all parts with some of the treated water. You do not want to miss treating any surface that may come into contact with your mouth or the water you are drinking.

WATER FILTERING DEVICES

There are a number of compact water filtration units that can give the backcountry traveler safe water for cooking. One device that I use regularly is a pump filtration unit made by Katadyn. It has been proven to filter out giardia and other harmful threats and the unit fits into a pack easily. Sweetwater and Pur make equally effective filtration systems.

A pump-type water filter should be an equipment must for all backcountry trips.

GETTING WATER UNDER FRIGID CONDITIONS

Any time you are traveling under frigid conditions, you should take along a reliable stove. Once you have the stove going, look for sources of water. Whenever possible, melt ice for water rather than snow. You get more water for the volume with less heat and time. Remember snow is seventeen parts air and one part water. If you melt snow by heating, put in a little snow at a time and compress it, or the pot will burn. If water is available, put a little in the bottom of the pot and add snow gradually.

Glacial ice gives roughly twice the water per fuel unit in half the time that snow does when melted. In addition, snow more often contains dirt, soot, and animal and human contaminants.

Do not try to eat ice or snow. A day or two of taking water in this manner produces a swollen, raw mucous membrane in the mouth, which may become painful enough to prevent eating or drinking until the inflammation subsides. Dogs eat snow and get away with it; humans cannot.

Once you have water, give it the boiling treatment.

GETTING SEDIMENT OUT OF WATER

If clear water is not available take the following steps:

1. Filter the water to be treated through a clean handkerchief or similar fabric.
2. Let the filtered water stand until any remaining sediment has settled to the bottom.
3. Pour off the clear water into the vessel in which you plan to treat it.
4. Treat the water.

Backcountry Drinks

Most of the drinks that are now found in the backcountry are instant powders that, when added to cold or hot water, magically become coffee, tea, chocolate, or orange juice. In fact, just this past year I was teaching a backpacking class in which most of the students thought that sassafras tea was a fictitious drink—a myth. On another occasion, I packed in a family of trout fisherman to a high lake on the Colorado Continental Divide. After helping them get their camp in order, I showed them their supplies for the coming week. In the grub box was a can of coffee and a large camp coffeepot. As I was about to leave, the wife called me over to the side to confess that the only coffee she had ever made was instant coffee, and she wanted to know how to make camp coffee—the real stuff.

As I said in the introduction, one of my reasons for writing this book was to record those age-old cooking techniques that are fast being forgotten but may be needed again soon. Brewing backcountry drinks is one technique worth saving.

With this in mind here are some of the old-time favorites and one or two new ones.

CAMP COFFEE

Select a coffeepot that best suits your needs in size. Fill the pot with a measured amount of cold water. Bring the water to a boil, then add 1 rounded tablespoon of coffee grounds for each cup of water and 1 for the pot. Stir and remove from heat. Pour in ½ cup cold water for every 10 cups of hot water to settle the grounds. The way most cooks with whom I have traveled settle the grounds is by tossing an eggshell into the pot. That method works just as well as cold water.

TRAIL TEA

Up in the Northwest Territories where I like to spend as much time as possible, the local natives carry a bag of loose tea. Just as soon as the dog sled has stopped, they start a fire and have tea. This is a tradition in the North Country and I find myself catching the habit after a few days on the trail. Here is how to make trail tea.

Into a pot of boiling water, add 1 level teaspoon of tea to 1 quart of water. (This makes mild tea. Add more tea for a stronger drink.) Do not boil tea. Remove from the fire at once and allow to steep from 5 to 7 minutes, depending on how hot you like your tea.

SPICE TEA

This is a quick-energy tea that I especially like when snowshoeing or cross-country skiing.

1 large jar Tang (1 lb. 2 oz.)　　*1 teaspoon cinnamon*
¾ cup instant tea with lemon　　*½ teaspoon ground cloves*
3 cups sugar

Mix above ingredients together well. Store in covered container, tightly sealed. To make tea, mix 3 teaspoons of this mixture with 1 cup boiling water.

TOMATO JUICE

Here is how you can have tomato juice in the backcountry while saving space and weight. To 1 quart of cold water, add 1 small can of tomato paste. Mix thoroughly and add 1 level teaspoon of salt and 1 level teaspoon of sugar.

APPLE JUICE

This is a good way to have apple juice and stewed apples at the same time. To 1 quart of cold water, add 1 cup of dried apples. Stew apples for 40 minutes. After removing from fire, drain the juice into a cup. Add sugar to taste and allow to cool.

BOUILLON DRINK

An old European drink that is nutritious and easy to make is a hot beef or chicken bouillon. Bouillon comes in cubes, powder form, and individual serving packages. Add 1 cube, 1 teaspoon of powder, or 1 package to 1 cup of hot water. It is a good, lightweight trail drink.

SASSAFRAS TEA

The sassafras (*Sassafras albidum*) tree, which is found throughout the eastern United States, is an excellent source for tea stock. During the fall or winter, dig a few roots at the base of a sassafras tree; if done in moderation, you will not hurt the tree. My dad has been getting his tea roots from the same tree for thirty years, and the tree is alive and well. Wash the roots and chop into small pieces. Boil in water until a pale reddish color is achieved. Sweeten the tea to taste and serve hot or cold. In the spring the leaves of the sassafras tree can also be gathered and then sun dried. The dried leaves, when added to boiling water, make a mild tea.

SUMAC LEMONADE

The staghorn sumac (*Rhus typhina*) bush, easily recognized by its stout, velvety twigs, has a pinnacle of red fruit in the fall. These red berries can be dried and stored for making a lemon-tasting drink. Place 1 cluster of berries in a small pan. Cover with boiling water and let sit for 5 minutes. Strain into a cup through a cloth. Sweeten to taste and serve cold. Be sure you know how to identify this plant before you go into the field. Many similar looking plants are poisonous.

ROSE HIP TEA

There are more than 35 varieties of wild roses found in North America. The fruit of the rose, commonly called rose hip, is rich in vitamin C. In fact, I am told that the rose hip has 50 times more vitamin C than an orange, by volume.

Pick the hips in early fall and dry outdoors in the shade or indoors at room temperature. To make the tea, grind or crush dried hips. Use 1 teaspoon for each cup of tea. Steep the tea for 10 to 15 minutes. Herb teas generally do not contain caffeine or tannic acid, so they can be steeped longer than Oriental teas. You obtain more flavor with longer steeping and also more vitamin value. Since the flavor of rose hip tea is mild, you may wish to add cinnamon and clove, a mint leaf or a curl of dried orange peel.

Cooking at High Elevations

One of the things our westward-moving forebears had to learn was how to cook at higher elevations. They suddenly realized that boiling water in the high passes of the Rocky Mountains was much different from that at the lower elevations of the plains. Today when wilderness wandering takes people into the high country, they must make some adjustments in cooking techniques. This is particularly true if they are depending upon freeze-dried food, which requires boiling water.

The major difference between high and low elevations (other than the altitude) is atmospheric pressure. The air pressure is greatest at sea level and becomes comparatively less the higher the elevation. At high elevations, water boils at a lower temperature than at sea level because it is under less pressure. (For instance, water boils at 212°F at sea level and 194°F at 10,000 feet above.) This simply means that food requiring boiling water takes longer to cook—approximately 10 percent longer per 1000 feet. Food requiring ten minutes of boiling time at sea level will need twenty minutes on a mountaintop with an elevation of 10,000 feet above sea level. Therefore, any food that is made with boiling water, such as all freeze-dried foods, should be tested for doneness by tasting often after ten minutes.

This same atmospheric pressure can affect anything that requires baking powder. For instance, our bannock mix normally calls for one teaspoon of baking powder; however, at 7500 feet above sea level this measurement would need to be decreased to three-fourth teaspoon, and at 10,000 feet to only one-half teaspoon. Otherwise you would have bannock the size of a basketball.

Other yeast breads and sourdough at high elevations will require shorter rising time. A good rule to follow is to allow the bread to rise to twice its original size.

As Paul Petzold, famous Wyoming mountain climber, once put it, "A meal that takes thirty minutes at sea level will never get cooked at high altitudes."

Suppliers

WHERE TO WRITE OR E-MAIL

Backpack Stoves
The Coleman Company—Peak I
3600 N. Hydraulic
Wichita, KS 67219
www.coleman.com

Cook Kits
Mirro Aluminum Co.
1512 Washington St.
Manitowoc, WI 54220
www.mirro.com

Dutch Ovens
Lodge Manufacturing Co.
P.O. Box 380
S. Pittsburg, TN 37380
www.lodgemfg.com

Reflector Oven and Sheepherders Stoves
Sims Stoves
P.O. Box 21405
Billings, MT 59104
www.wtp.net/simsstov

Smokers

Masterbuilt Mfg. Co.
450 Brown Ave.
Columbus, GA 31906

The Brinkman Corp.
4215 McEwen Rd.
Dallas, TX 75244

Commercial Food Dehydrators

Excalibur
6083 Power Inn Rd.
Sacramento, CA 95824

Camp Stove Ovens

Fox Hill Corp.
P.O. Box 259
Rozet, WY 85727
www.foxhill.net

Catalog Houses

Cabela's
400 E. Ave. A
Oshkosh, NE 69190
www.cabelas.com

Campmor
P.O. Box 700-K
Saddle River, NJ 07458
www.campmor.com

Forestry Suppliers, Inc.
P.O. Box 8397
Jackson, MS 39284
www.forestry-suppliers.com

Alaskan Jerky, 83–84
Apples:
  Apple Juice, 130–31
  Breakfast Apples, 28
  Dutch Oven Apple Surprise, 39
  Hardtack, 88–89
Apricot Shortcake, 69

Badlands Goulash, 55
Baked Fish, 47
Baked Potatoes, 29
Baked Rattlesnake, 40
Baked Spam, 48
Banana Dessert, 30
Bannock:
  Basic, 63
  Bread, 65–66
  Cabin Cake, 68
  Cinnamon Rolls, 68
  Fish Sticks, 67
  Hamburger Pie, 67
  Pancakes, 66
  Strawberry Shortcake, 67–68
Basic Gorp, 90
Beans:
  Bean Delight, 28–29
  Bean Hole Beans, 122

Beef and Beans, 54
Dutch Oven Beans, 39
Hikers' Beans, 57
Beef:
  Bannock Hamburger Pie, 67
  Beef and Beans, 54
  Beef Jerky, 83
  Beef Stew with Bannock Dumplings, 66–67
  Beer Burgers, 115
  Campfire Meat Loaf, 46
  Camphouse Roast Beef, 116
  Chipped Beef on Biscuits, 53
  Cowpoke Spaghetti, 58
  Frypan Burgwiches, 58
  High Sierra Skillet, 59
  Hobo Stew, 29
  Homesteader's Jerky, 84
  Hurry Hash, 53
  Panhandle Chili, 55
  Quick Stew, 53
  Ranger's Rice with Beef Seasoned Jerky, 57
  Skewered Beef Balls, 115
  Smoked Jerky, 85
  Sportsman's Jerky, 85–86
  Sweet Jerky, 85
  Trail Spaghetti, 58

Bouillon Drink, 131
Boulettes, 60–61
Breads:
Bannock Bread, 65–66
Sourdough Bread, 75–76
Sourdough French Bread, 76
Sourdough Muffins, 75
Sourdough Wheat, 76–77
Survival Bread, 91–92
Breakfast Apples, 28
Brunswick Stew, 38
Butterscotch-Chocolate
Frosting, 78

Cabin Jerky, 80–81
Cake:
Apricot Shortcake, 69
Bannock Cabin Cake, 68
Bannock Cinnamon Rolls, 68
Bannock Strawberry
Shortcake, 67–68
Cherry Cake, 46–47
Johnny Cake, 56–57
Oatcakes, 91
Sourdough Chocolate Cake,
77
Tater Knob Hoecake, 38
Camp Coffee, 129–30
Campfire Meat Loaf, 46
Campfire Tuna, 55
Camphouse Roast Beef, 116
Camp Shrimp, 29
Campsite Gravy, 60
Cheese, Smoked, 103–104
Cherry Cake, 46–47
Chicken:
Chicken Dinners in a
Package, 117
Meat Pies, 48
Chipped Beef on Biscuits, 53

Cinnamon:
Bannock Cinnamon Rolls, 68
Cinnamon Toast, 46
Coffee, Camp, 129–30
Compass Franks, 59
Corn:
and Frank Chowder, 56
Chowder, 54
-on-the-Cob, 29
Parched, 89
Cowpoke spaghetti, 60

Duck á l'Orange, 104
Dutch Oven Apple Surprise, 39
Dutch Oven Baked Fish, 39
Dutch Oven Beans, 39
Dutch Oven Venison, 40–41

Eggs, Roundup Scrambled, 59
Expedition Mix, 92

Fish:
Baked, 47
Bannock Fish Sticks, 67
Campfire Tuna, 55
Camp Shrimp, 29
Dutch Oven Baked, 39
Foil, 28
Garfish Court Bouillon, 61
Garfish Patties, 60–61
Grilled Fillets, 116–17
Smoked, 104–105
Smoked Oysters, 105
Smoked Salmon, 106–107
Tip-Top Tuna, 54
Foil Fish, 28
Frankfurters:
Compass Franks, 59
Corn and Frank Chowder,
56

Wrapped Dogs, 47–48
Fruit Leather, 90
Frypan Burgwiches, 58

Garfish Court Bouillon, 61
Garfish Patties, 60–61
Good Night Special, 60
Gorp, Basic, 90
Goulash, Bad Lands, 54
Granola, 90–91
Grilled Fish Fillets, 116–17
Grilled Pork Chops, 116
Grilled Turkey, 114

Ham:
    and Red Eye Gravy, 56
    Hurry Hash, 53
    Meat Pies, 48
Hardtack, 88–89
High Sierra Skillet, 59
Hikers' Beans, 57
Hobo Stew, 29
Homesteader's Jerky, 84
Hurry Hash, 53

Jerky:
    Alaskan, 83–84
    Basic, 80
    Beef, 83
    Cabin, 80–81
    Homesteader's, 84
    Quick, 81
    Salmon, 86
    Salted, 82
    Seasoned, 82
    Smoked, 85
    Sportsman's, 85–86
    Sweet, 85
    Venison, 82–83
Johnny Cake, 56–57

Lemonade, Sumac, 131

Meat Pies, 48
Modern Pemmican, 88
Mountain Chowder, 58
Muesli, 91

Oatcakes, 91
Original Pemmican, 88
Oven-Dried Fruit, 97
Oven-Dried Vegetables, 97–98

Pancakes Sourdough, 74–75
Panhandle Chili, 55
Parched Corn, 89
Pemmican:
    Modern, 88
    Original, 88
Pioneer Soup, 57
Pork Chops, Grilled, 116
Potatoes, Baked, 29
Pumpkin Seeds, Roasted, 89

Quail:
    Roasted with Mushrooms, 47
    Sherried, 39
Quick Jerky, 81
Quick Stew, 53

Rangers' Rice with Beef, 57
Rattlesnake, Baked, 40
Roasted Pumpkin Seeds, 90
Roasted Quail with
    Mushrooms, 47
Roasted Soybeans, 89
Rose Hip Tea, 131–32
Roundup Scrambled Eggs, 59

Salmon Jerky, 86
Salted Jerky, 82

Sassafras Tea, 131
Seasoned Jerky, 82
Sherried Quail, 39
Skewered Beef Balls, 115
Smoked Cheese, 103–104
Smoked Fish, 104–105
Smoked Jerky, 85
Smoked Nuts, 103
Smoked Oysters, 105
Smoked Salmon, 106–107
Smoked Salt, 104
Snacks:
    Basic Gorp, 90
    Expedition Mix, 92
    Fruit Leather, 90
    Granola, 90–91
    Hardtack, 88–89
    Modern Pemmican, 88
    Muesli, 91
    Original Pemmican, 88
    Parched Corn, 89
    Roasted Pumpkin Seed, 89
    Roasted Soybeans, 89
    Smoked Cheese, 103–104
    Smoked Nuts, 103
    Sweet Balls, 48
Soups:
    Beef Stew with Bannock
        Dumplings, 66–67
    Brunswick Stew, 38
    Corn and Frank Chowder, 56
    Corn Chowder, 54
    Hobo Stew, 29
    Mountain Chowder, 58
    Panhandle Chili, 55
    Pioneer, 57
    Quick Stew, 53
    Venison Stew, 40
Sourdough:
    Bread, 75–76

Chocolate Cake, 77
French Bread, 76
Muffins, 75
Pancakes, 74–75
Starter, 72–74
Waffles, 75
Wheat, 76–77
Soybeans, Roasted, 89
Spam, Baked, 48
Spice Tea, 130
Sportsman's Jerky, 85–86
Sumac Lemonade, 131
Sun-Dried Fruit, 95
Sun-Dried Vegetables,
    95–97
Survival Bread, 91–92
Sweet Balls, 48
Sweet Jerky, 85

Tater Knob Hoecake, 38
Tea:
    Rose Hip Tea, 131–32
    Sassafras Tea, 131
    Spice Tea, 130
    Trail Tea, 130
Tip-Top Tuna, 54
Tomato Juice, 130
Trail Spaghetti, 58
Turkey:
    Grilled Turkey, 114
    Meat Pies, 48

Venison:
    Dutch Oven Venison,
        40–41
    Sportsman's Jerky, 85–86
    Venison Jerky, 82–83
    Venison Stew, 40

Wrapped Dogs, 47–48

Index

alcohol for backpack stove, 5
aluminum cookware, cleaning, 17
aluminum foil, cooking with, 1, 25–30
  charcoal grill, lining the, 111
  cooking fire for, 28
  equipment for, 28
  heavy-duty vs. lightweight, 26
  recipes for, 28–30
atmospheric pressure, effect on
  cooking of, 133–34

backcountry drinks, 129–32
backpack stoves:
  as backup stove for home use, 7
  cook set for, 7
  fuel container for, 7
  fuel types for, 5–6
  illustration, 2, 6
  learning to use at home, 7
  suppliers, 135
  ventilation for home use, 7
  versatility of, 2–3
baking:
  with Dutch oven, 34–35
  with reflector oven, 43–48
  in sheepherder's stove, 52–53
bannock, 63–69
  recipes, 64–69
basting brush, 109
bean hole cooking, 119–22
Blume, Lloyd, 71
boiling water, 124
bow saw, 17
bread:
  cooking on a spit, 22
  sourdough, 3

broiling with rock broiler, 24
butane for backpack stove, 5

campfires, 11–15
  firewood for, 13
  keyhole fire, 12
  leaving the site, preparations for,
    14–15
  safety, 14
  site for, 11–12
  tinder for, 13–14
Campways backpack cook set, 7
catalog houses, list of, 136
chain saw, 18–19
charcoal, cooking with, 109–17
  cooking tools for, 109
  grilling, see charcoal grill
  making your own charcoal, 111
  with permanent fire pit, 109
  recipes for, 114–17
charcoal briquettes, 111
  for baking in Dutch oven, 34–35
  saving partially burned, 111, 112
  selecting, 110
charcoal grill, 109–13
  building too large a fire, 112
  decreasing heat of fire, 112
  flare-ups, stopping, 112
  hamburgers that fall apart on, 113
  illustration, 2
  increasing heat of fire, 112
  lining, with aluminum foil, 111
  mistakes of novices, 112
  prolonging the life of, 113
  recipes for, 114–17
  safety, 112

charcoal grill *(cont.)*
   site for, 109–10
   starting the fire, 111, 112
   storage of, 113
   testing the temperature of coals,
      112
   time to wait between starting fire
      and cooking, 111–12
   windshield, 110
cholera, 124
Clorox, treating water with, 124–25
Coleman Company, 6
cooking fire, building a, 11–19
   campfire, *see* campfires
   cutting tools, firewood, 17–18
   fireplace fire, 15–17
   firewood for, 14–15, 16–17, 19
   in the snow, 14
cooking without utensils, 3, 21–24
Cooperative Extension Service,
      University of Alaska, 72
cutting tools, firewood, 17–19

dehydration, 123
dehydrators, commercial food, 98,
      136
dried food:
   commercial dehydrators, 98, 136
   as fastest growing method of food
      preservation, 93
   fruits, oven-dried, 97
   history of, 93
   making your own, 93–100
   meat, *see* jerky
   oven drying, 97–98
   storage space conserved by, 93
   sun drying, 93, 94–97
   vegetables, oven—dried, 97–98
      chart, 99–100
drinks, backcountry, 129–32
Dutch oven, 1, 31–41
   aluminum, 32
   baking with, 34–35
   cast iron, 31
   cleaning, 33, 34
   fireplace cooking with, 1, 2, 15,
      36–37
   frying, using the lid for, 34, 35
   getting the lid to seat property,
      32–33
   history of use of, 31–32
   illustration, 2

preparing for use, 33–34
   purchasing of, 32
   recipes, 38–41
   size of, 32
   slow, unattended cooking with, 37
   "stack cooking," 35, 36
   suppliers, 135
   "sweetening" methods, 33
   tools to use with, 35–36
   versatility of, 33
dysentery, 124

eggs, rock broiler for cooking, 24
electric starter, 111
elevation, cooking at high, 133–34
Excalibur Dehydrator, 98

fireplace:
   building a cooking fire, 15–17
   chart evaluating, 19
   cooking in the, 1, 15–17
      with Dutch oven, 1, 2, 15, 36–37
      with reflector oven, 15, 43
   glass doors, 16
   ventilation, 16
fireplace poker, 35–36
fires, cooking, *see* cooking fire,
      building a
firewood:
   for cooking fires, 13–15, 16–17, 19
   green wood, 16, 103
   hardwoods, 13, 15
   kindling, 15
   resinous, 17
   for smoking foods, 102
   softwoods, 13, 16, 102
   tinder, 13–14
   unseasoned, 16
fish:
   cooking without utensils, 22, 24
   smoking, 105–106
Fox Hill Outfitters, 52
Franklin stoves, 16
freeze-dried foods, 7
   bagging foods by meal, 8
   cost control, 8
   expense of, 8
   following the instructions for, 7
   meal planning, 8
   packaging your own, 8
   variety of, 7–8
   water needs, planning for, 8–9

French, Pam and Ken, 119, 122
fruits, oven-dried, 97
frying, Dutch oven lid for, 34, 35

gasoline:
  as fire starter, caution against using,
    14, 112
  white gasoline, for backpack stove,
    5–6
giardia, 124
green wood, 16, 103
Gresham, Tom, 102
grill scraper, 109
gypsy spit, 22

halazone tablets, 125
hardwoods, 13, 15
high elevations, cooking at, 133–34
Holm, Don, 72

ice, melting, for water, 126–27
iodine treatment of water, 125

jack saw, 17
jerky, 87
  cuts of meat for, 80
  history as trail food, 79
  making your own, 79–86
  recipes, 80–86
  as staple of Native Americans, 3, 87

Katadyn, 125
kerosene for backpack stove, 5
keyhole fire, 12
kindling, 15

Lewis and Clark expedition, 2, 32, 87

MacKenzie, Alexander, 87
Master-Built charcoal-gas-fired
    smoker, 101
meat:
  for jerky, 80
  smoking, 22–23

Native Americans:
  drying of foods by, 93
  jerky as staple of, 3, 87
  smoking of foods, 105
Neal, Jake, 51
Northrop, Medrick, 13

oak, 13, 102

Peary, Admiral, 87
pemmican, 87
  recipes, 88
Petzold, Paul, 134
Portable-Aqua tablets, 125
pot holders, 109
propane for backpack stove, 5
Pur water filtration system, 125

recipes, *see recipe index* (page 137)
reflector oven, 2, 3
  from aluminum foil, 45
  baking with, 43–48
  fireplace cooking with, 15, 43
  firewood for cooking fire, 46
  illustration, 2
  optimum fire for, 45
  principle behind, 45
  recipes for, 46–48
  suppliers, 135
  temperature of, guessing the,
    45–46
  two, use of, 45
Revere, Paul, 31
rock broiler, 24
rock oven, 23–24
Roughing It Easy (Thomas), 45

saws, 17–19
sediment in water, removing, 127
sheepherder's stove, 3, 49–61
  advantages of, 51
  cooking on, 52–53
  dampers, 51
  history of, 49
  illustration, 2
  mail-order sales of, 49
  preparations for using, 52
  recipes for, 53–61
  safe use of, 51
  Sims Sportsman, 49–50
  stop top oven, 52–53
  suppliers, 135
  tent, use in a, 51
  top of, used as griddle, 52
shovel, 35, 109
Sims, P. D., 49
Sims Sportsman, 49–50
smoke-hole cooking, 22–23
smokehouses, 100

smoker:
  illustration, 2
  suppliers, 136
smoking food, 100–107
  aromatic woods for, 102
  commercial smoker, 101–105
    recipes for, 103–105
  improvised smoker, 105–106
    recipe, 106–107
snow, 127
  building a cooking fire in the, 14
  making a campfire in the, 14
softwoods, 13, 16
sourdough bread, 71–78, 134
  Alaskan gold miners and, 3
  recipes, 72–78
  starter, 3, 72
spark arrester, 51
spit, 21–22
suppliers, list of, 135–36
Sweetwater filtration system, 125

Thomas, Diane, 45
tinder, 13–14
tongs, 109, 112
trail foods:
  jerky, *see* jerky
  recipes, 88–92
twisted-toothed wire saw, 17
typhoid, 124

U.S. Forest Service, 15
utensils, primitive cooking without, 3,
  21–24

vegetables, oven-dried, 97–98
  chart, 99–100
ventilation:
  for backstove use in the home, 7
  of charcoal grill, 110
  fireplace, 16

water:
  boiling, 124
  Clorox treatment, 124–25
  commercial tablets to purify, 125
  daily requirements, 123
  diseases from impure, 124
  filtering devices, 125–26
  under frigid conditions, getting,
    126–27
  iodine treatment, 125
  making it safe for drinking, 123–27
  myths about purifying, 123–24
  planning for your needs, 8–9
  purifying, 124–25
  removing sediment form, 127
  treatment methods, 124–25
  from unknown source, 124
whiskbroom, 36
white gasoline for backpack stove,
  5–6
wood stove, cooking on the, 1, 2

MORE WILDERNESS RECIPES

Ingredients:

_____   _____

_____   _____

_____   _____

_____   _____

_____   _____

_____

Instructions:

Ingredients:

_____   _____

_____   _____

_____   _____

_____   _____

_____   _____

_____   _____

Instructions:

_____

_____

_____

_____

_____

_____

_____

_____

_____

_____

_____

_____

_____

_____

Ingredients:

_____   _____
_____   _____
_____   _____
_____   _____
_____   _____
_____   _____

Instructions:

_____
_____
_____
_____
_____
_____
_____
_____
_____
_____
_____
_____
_____
_____
_____
_____

Ingredients:

_____   _____

_____   _____

_____   _____

_____   _____

_____   _____

Instructions:

_____

_____

_____

_____

_____

_____

_____

_____

_____

_____

_____

_____

_____

_____

_____